JOAN DIDION

MODERN LITERATURE SERIES

GENERAL EDITOR: Philip Winsor

In the same series:

S. Y. AGNON   *Harold Fisch*
SHERWOOD ANDERSON   *Welford Dunaway Taylor*
LEONID ANDREYEV   *Josephine M. Newcombe*
ISAAC BABEL   *R. W. Hallett*
JAMES BALDWIN   *Carolyn Wedin Sylvander*
SIMONE DE BEAUVOIR   *Robert Cottrell*
SAUL BELLOW   *Brigitte Scheer-Schäzler*
BERTOLT BRECHT   *Willy Haas*
JORGE LUIS BORGES   *George R. McMurray*
ALBERT CAMUS   *Carol Petersen*
TRUMAN CAPOTE   *Helen S. Garson*
WILLA CATHER   *Dorothy Tuck McFarland*
JOHN CHEEVER   *Samuel T. Coale*
COLETTE   *Robert Cottrell*
JOSEPH CONRAD   *Martin Tucker*
JULIO CORTÁZAR   *Evelyn Picon Garfield*
JOAN DIDION   *Katherine Usher Henderson*
JOHN DOS PASSOS   *George J. Becker*
THEODORE DREISER   *James Lundquist*
FRIEDRICH DÜRRENMATT   *Armin Arnold*
T. S. ELIOT   *Joachim Seyppel*
WILLIAM FAULKNER   *Joachim Seyppel*
F. SCOTT FITZGERALD   *Rose Adrienne Gallo*
FORD MADOX FORD   *Sondra J. Stang*
JOHN FOWLES   *Barry N. Olshen*
MAX FRISCH   *Carol Petersen*
ROBERT FROST   *Elaine Barry*
GABRIEL GARCÍA MÁRQUEZ   *George R. McMurray*
MAKSIM GORKI   *Gerhard Habermann*
GÜNTER GRASS   *Kurt Lothar Tank*
ROBERT GRAVES   *Katherine Snipes*
PETER HANDKE   *Nicholas Hern*
LILLIAN HELLMAN   *Doris V. Falk*
ERNEST HEMINGWAY   *Samuel Shaw*
HERMANN HESSE   *Franz Baumer*
CHESTER HIMES   *James Lundquist*
HUGO VON HOFMANNSTHAL   *Lowell W. Bangerter*
CHRISTOPHER ISHERWOOD   *Claude J. Summers*
SARAH ORNE JEWETT   *Josephine Donovan*
UWE JOHNSON   *Mark Boulby*

(continued on last page of book)

JOAN DIDION

Katherine Usher Henderson

FREDERICK UNGAR PUBLISHING CO.
NEW YORK

83-39395

To Tracy

Library of Congress Cataloging in Publication Data

Henderson, Katherine U.
    Joan Didion.
    (Modern literature series)
    Bibliography: p.
    Includes index.
    1. Didion, Joan—Criticism and interpretation.
PS3554.I33Z68   813'.54   80-53705
ISBN 0-8044-2370-9
ISBN 0-8044-6265-8 (pbk.)

Contents

Preface

Through analysis and interpretation of Joan Didion's novels and essays, this book aims to illuminate her writings for college students and the general reader. I have, however, used scholarly conventions where appropriate to place the writings in a broad critical and historical context. Because Didion is a peculiarly American writer, the context is primarily that of American culture and literature.

Didion's novels explore the moral dilemmas and the human failures resulting from the confrontation between traditional American values and a new social and political reality. Her fictional characters all inherit the legacy of the frontier experience; this legacy falls on them like white light on a prism, breaking into its component colors— blind faith in the future, commitment to the family, a conviction that hard work guarantees success. Then, as darkness shadows color, the violence of the contemporary experience exposes these values as myths, ideas as ephemeral as the rainbow. The darkness destroys some of her characters; others it pushes into madness. A few survive through sheer tenacity of will. But they all lose the prismatic colors of romantic optimism that came to them as a birthright.

In her essays, too, Didion defines the character of America through its heroes, achievements, failures and obsessions. She also defines herself: as a writer, as a member of a generation that shared certain attitudes, as a Californian, but preeminently as an American. So strong is this identification that when her nation suffers violence and aimlessness, she becomes ill herself, driven to the edge of madness by the vast chasm between her expectation of order and the chaotic reality.

Used as tools to chip away illusion, words are for Didion a defense against madness, for they discover and express her own essence as well as her vision of contemporary America. Her fierce personal and artistic integrity require that we have no illusions about her, just as she seeks to have none about us. In revealing her weaknesses, doubts and most stubborn values, she has left herself vulnerable to public scrutiny and criticism—and from critics who regard her revelations as posturing, she has felt disdain as well. But her relentless self-examination and uncompromisingly realistic portrayal of contemporary America have also won her critical acclaim and genuine admiration from readers who recognize the ultimate compliment in her assumption that they want above all the truth.

Acknowledgments

My principal debt in the writing of this monograph is to my colleague Barbara F. McManus, who brought to her reading of the manuscript a rich knowledge of the traditions of American literature so important to an understanding of Didion's work. Her suggestions also lent clarity and grace to many passages which lacked these qualities; any awkwardness remaining, however, is certainly mine.

I owe special thanks to the librarians of Gill Library of the College of New Rochelle for their generous assistance in locating the more elusive of Didion's uncollected pieces; to the College itself I am indebted for funding the typing of the manuscript. I am grateful to Ann and Chris Stone for acting as my guides through "Didion country." Finally, I wish to thank Carol Graziani and Marilyn Catania, graduate students who took time from their own work to help me with mine.

Chronology

best-seller, and is nominated for a National Book Award.

1971:   Didion and Dunne move to Trancas, a town on the Pacific Coast north of Los Angeles.

1975:   Didion is a visiting regents lecturer at Berkeley for a semester.

1977:   *A Book of Common Prayer* is published.

1978:   Didion and Dunne move to Brentwood Park, Los Angeles.

1979:   *The White Album*, Didion's second collection of essays, is published.

Joan Didion:
A Biographical Essay

In the study of her colonial home in Brentwood, Los Angeles, Didion has a framed photograph of the Sierra Nevada, a reminder of the Donner–Reed pioneers who, while traveling from Illinois to California in 1846, were forced by winter storms to make camp in these mountains. Of the eighty-seven members who left Illinois, forty survived—by eating their own dead. Nancy Hardin Cornwall, Didion's own great-great-great grandmother, was a member of the original Donner party, although she left the group in Nevada to take the northern route through Oregon to California.[1]

The story of the Donner–Reed experience is for Didion an emblem of the realistic, as opposed to the romantic, version of the westward migration in the United States. As a child growing up in Sacramento, where the sense of local history and patriotism was intense, Didion was exposed to revisionist history in which the founding of California was viewed as an act of unsurpassed heroism. She later wrote that "Such a view of history casts a certain melancholia over those who participate in it; my own childhood was suffused with the conviction that we had long outlived our finest hour."[2]

Didion's own attitude toward the Sacramento of her childhood is sharply ambivalent. She did feel the melancholy of its persistent backward glance, but she also took pride in the fact that the land on which she lived had belonged to her family for five generations. Her earliest memories, evocative of a child's sense of physical freedom, are of Sacramento's rivers and open land:

> . . . I remember running a boxer dog of my brother's over the same flat fields that our great-great-grandfather had found virgin and had planted; I remember swimming . . . the same rivers we had swum for a century: the Sacramento, so rich with silt that we could barely see our hands a few inches beneath the surface; the American, running clean and fast with melted Sierra snow until July. . . . sometimes the Cosumnes, occasionally the Feather.[3]

Despite these pastoral pleasures, Didion was not a carefree child. She was "afraid of sinkholes and afraid of snakes"[4] when swimming in the local rivers, and she had recurrent fantasies of disaster—the bridge over the Sacramento River falling, or cable cars dropping into Royal Gorge.[5] In her first story, written at the age of five, a woman who dreamed that she was freezing to death in the Arctic awoke to discover that she was in fact dying of heat on the Sahara Desert.[6] In certain moods the adult Didion is still obsessed with disaster, and the minds of depressed characters in her novels fasten on real or imagined catastrophe: Everett McClellan in *Run River* is tormented every year by fear of his harvested hops burning in the kiln in which they are stored, and Maria Wyeth in *Play It As It Lays* cannot forget the incident of two honeymooners killed by a coral snake while they slept in their Scout camper.

Far from attributing her fearfulness to childhood trauma, Didion insists that her childhood was normal and happy. Her father is a shy, quiet man whose family originally came from Alsace-Lorraine; an Army Air Corps finance officer during World War II, he is now involved in real estate. From the few glimpses she has afforded of her mother, one pictures a determined, civic-minded woman; we know that she was active in the

Sacramento community, serving successive terms on the school board. Straightforward in manner, she is probably less conventional than most Sacramento matrons; when she met John Dunne for the first time at Joan's wedding, she presented herself to him as one of "those little old ladies in tennis shoes you've heard about."[7]

Although Didion has written about the meaning of "home" to her at different times in her life, she has never characterized in her writings either her parents or her younger brother Jimmy (her only sibling). This reticence about her family may derive in part from a respect for their privacy, but it certainly also derives from her conviction that we are molded less by our personal interaction with our parents than by our genes, our biochemistry, and our historical time and place.

Thus, while Didion's family are shadowy figures in her writing, the Sacramento of her childhood is sharply defined, both in her essays and in her first novel, *Run River*. Didion located the pulse of Sacramento not in the town, but in the river ranches where hops were grown and in the fruit ranches whose pears and oranges were shipped across the country. "In what way does the Holy Land resemble the Sacramento Valley?" she was asked by her Episcopalian Sunday school teacher, and the answer was, "In the type and diversity of its agricultural products."[8] The valley is, according to Didion, "the richest and most intensely cultivated agricultural region in the world, a giant outdoor hot-house with a billion-dollar crop."[9] But her Sunday school teacher was teaching more than facts; she was hinting that the valley was sacred, a fertile Eden.

The Sacramento Valley is splendid in its natural beauty, but it was its provincial insulation from the outside world that contributed most strongly to the persistence of this Edenic myth. Few people moved into the valley, and fewer still moved out. Most of the families Didion knew had been long resident; sixth generation herself, she spent her weekends visiting "dozens of great-

aunts, year after year of Sundays."[10] The myth main-
tained that permanent residents were magically protected
from evil; according to Didion's grandmother, only
visiting children drowned in the local rivers.

It is difficult to determine in what spirit Didion
understood this myth as a child. She probably heard the
false note sounded, for she knew local children who
drowned in the rivers and knew, too, the destruction that
threatened when the spring rains swelled the rivers until a
levee burst. However, the valley was for a long time the
most stable world she knew. Thus it seems unlikely that
the myth dissolved for her before adulthood. In *Run River*,
her novel of the valley written while she was living and
working in New York, a whole generation is entrapped by
the notion of the valley as an immutable Eden; the
families in the novel are unable either to leave or to endure the changes wrought by the postwar intrusion of the
outside world. Perhaps fragments of the myth cling to her
still; she has returned to Sacramento, to the room she
lived in as a child, to write the final chapters of all three of
her novels.

During World War II Didion was expelled from this
paradise, while her family followed her father about the
country from one Air Corps base to another. In three
years, the family moved four times, settling for brief
periods in three different states: Washington, North
Carolina, and Colorado. She has written little about these
years, but they must have been difficult for the sensitive
eight-year-old who imagined sweeping disasters even
before the bombs fell on Pearl Harbor. On that occasion
she was shown Pearl Harbor in an atlas; for a long time
after that Hawaii to her "meant war and my father going
away and makeshift Christmases in rented rooms . . .
and nothing the same ever again."[11] It is not surprising
that she had her first migraine headache (she has had
them regularly ever since) while her father was stationed
at Peterson Field in Colorado Springs; the fire drill at

school, which immediately preceded the headache, must have felt ominous to a child already dislocated by war.[12] Her only record of a neutral time during this period is found in an essay on John Wayne, an actor she discovered in the summer of 1943, when she and her brother, for lack of other diversion, spent afternoons watching movies in a Quonset hut.

When the war ended, Didion and her family returned to Sacramento. It was a long time before Joan regained the sense of belonging that she had felt as a small child, however. A few years after her return she began writing stories the invariable theme of which was suicide; these stories probably reflected her own sadness and isolation. Her protagonists disposed of themselves either by jumping off a high bridge or by walking into the sea. The summer that she was thirteen, her parents rented a cottage at the beach, and she decided to experiment with suicidal behavior herself. One dark night, note pad in hand, she slowly entered the Pacific Ocean. The wave that knocked her over made note-taking difficult, however, and so far as we know this was her single experiment with watery self-destruction.[13]

During junior high school Didion must have been alone a good deal; close friends do not appear in her recollections of this period. Beginning in her early teens, she developed instead a profound affinity for literature that has been perhaps the most constant and reassuring relationship of her life. She not only wrote stories; she also typed whole chapters from the fiction of Conrad and Hemingway. When asked in 1977 what authors influenced her style, Didion mentioned Conrad and James but stressed Hemingway above all others: ". . . I was very influenced by Hemingway when I was 13, 14, 15. I learned a lot about how . . . a short sentence worked in a paragraph, how a long sentence worked. . . . How every word had to matter."[14]

At C. K. McClatchy Senior High School, Didion

seems to have been less alone. In the evenings she and her friends often drove down to the river, where they sat on the levee, "drinking vodka-and-orange-juice and listening to Les Paul and Mary Ford and their echoes . . . on the car radio."[15] Together with Nina Warren, daughter of the California governor, she belonged to a sorority called the Mañana Club which met in the Governor's Mansion, an old Victorian Gothic house spacious enough to accommodate sixty adolescent girls without disrupting the household routine. During an initiation rite Didion was characterized by Nina as "stuck on herself"; at that moment, she says, "I learned for the first time that my face to the world was not necessarily the face in my mirror."[16]

While her statements about her high school years are incidental, occurring in essays on other subjects, Didion has written at some length about her social and intellectual experience from 1952 to 1956 at the University of California at Berkeley. Her most compelling memories of college are of her relationships with literature and with herself. "I remember my real joy at discovering how language worked, at discovering, for example, that the central line of *Heart of Darkness* was a postscript."[17] Unhappy with the group life of her sorority, during her junior and senior years she lived in a bare apartment and read Camus and Henry James. She was not a uniformly brilliant student, for the abstract ideas of science and philosophy simply did not engage her mind like a sharp visual image or sensory impression:

I would try to contemplate the Hegelian dialectic and would find myself concentrating instead on a flowering pear tree outside my window and the particular way the petals fell on my floor. I would try to read linguistic theory and would find myself wondering instead if the lights were on in the bevatron up the hill.[18]

One should not infer that Didion could not handle abstractions—many of her finest essays are definitions of abstract qualities—but it is the nature of her mind to begin with a concrete image or series of images and then analyze their meaning ("Why have the night lights in the bevatron burned in my mind for twenty years?"[19]). Her mental processes are purely inductive, for she reasons always from the particular to the general, from the concrete example to the abstract principle which it illustrates. Inevitably, Didion majored in English literature, the discipline that enabled her to analyze the rendering of concrete sensory experience in patterns of language and imagery that give it larger meaning.

Didion claims that many of her adult attitudes and expectations took shape at Berkeley among that "silent generation" of students who did not seek to remedy social injustice, but rather tried to find a place for themselves in a society that they assumed to be imperfect because imperfection was fundamental to the nature of man. Didion has written in defense of this generation, arguing that its silence bespoke wisdom rather than cowardice:

. . . we were silent neither, as some thought, because we shared the period's official optimism nor, as others thought, because we feared its official repression. We were silent because the exhilaration of social action seemed to many of us just one more way of escaping the personal, of masking for a while that dread of the meaninglessness which was man's fate.[20]

Eloquent and succinct, this passage no doubt describes accurately the overt social attitudes of Didion and her classmates. On an emotional level, however, Didion clearly shared to some degree the "official optimism" of the period. In her famous essay on self-respect, she lists some of the illusions that she relinquished after the shock of her failure to be elected to Phi Beta Kappa:

I lost the conviction that lights would always turn green for me, the pleasant certainty that those rather passive virtues which had won me approval as a child guaranteed me not only Phi Beta Kappa keys but happiness, honor, and the love of a good man;

lost a certain touching faith in the totem power of good manners, clean hair, and proven competence on the Stanford-Binet scale.[21]

Although she might have believed intellectually that each person must confront alone a meaningless universe, at the same time she shared the view of an entire generation of middle-class college women that love and happiness (in the form of children and "a good man") would be no more difficult than getting into college, and were in fact a "right" earned through intelligence and ladylike behavior. While Didion was able by 1961 to define these illusions, it seems unlikely that she could readily shed them, so deeply were they embedded in postwar American culture. Indeed, she fully realized their tragic potential; in each of her three major novels the heroine nurtures the fantasy that she need not be assertive or reflective to gain happiness and success, since these rewards are an inalienable right of the well-bred American citizen.

In her senior year Didion took first place in *Vogue*'s Prix de Paris contest for young writers with an article on the San Francisco architect William Wilson Wurster. Given the choice of a trip to Paris or a job on the magazine, she chose the latter. At the time of this decision, she had been to New York only once, in the summer of 1955. On that occasion she was both captivated and overwhelmed by the size and sophistication of the city:

That first night I opened my window on the bus into town and watched for the skyline, but all I could see were . . . the big signs that said MIDTOWN TUNNEL THIS LANE and then a flood of summer rain (even that seemed remarkable and exotic, for I had come out of the West where there was no summer rain), and for the next three days I sat wrapped in blankets in a hotel room air-conditioned to 35° and tried to get over a bad cold and a high fever.[22]

She knew of no doctor she could call and was afraid to ask that the air conditioner be turned off because such a request would require her to figure out how much of a tip this favor warranted.

To consider Didion's temperament and the place where she spent her girlhood is to wonder that she came to New York at all. In Sacramento New York City was considered uncivilized, almost barbaric; people she knew felt it not worth a visit and unthinkable as a place of residence. She was temperamentally shy and fearful of making the most simple demands upon people. It was not primarily the job at *Vogue* that brought her there, for there were jobs in California, too, and, according to her own testimony, she did not yet know that she was a writer.

Didion's principal motive for coming to New York was a compelling need to understand all possible varieties of felt experience. It was the same motive that drove her to walk into the dark ocean at the age of thirteen, and the same that in future years would draw her to scenes of pain and confusion—drug addicted flower children in Haight-Ashbury, the burial of American soldiers in Hawaii, the Manson murders. In explaining why she loved New York, Didion wrote of the kinds of experience it afforded her:

I remember walking across Sixty-second Street one twilight that first spring. . . . I was late to meet someone but I stopped at Lexington Avenue and bought a peach. . . . I could taste the peach and feel the soft air blowing from a subway grating on my legs and I could smell lilac and garbage and expensive perfume. . . .

. . . Just around every corner lay something curious and interesting, something I had never before seen or done or known about.[23]

She went to every party to which she was invited, and, although her manner was diffident, she came to know both people at the center of the "literary scene" and those who existed on its fringes. She believed passionately in meeting "new faces" and advocated parties as a tonic for friends who were depressed. Her work gave orderly routine to her life:

I liked . . . the soothing and satisfactory rhythm of getting out a magazine. . . . I liked all the minutiae of proofs and layouts, liked working late on the nights the magazine went to press, sitting and reading *Variety* and waiting for the copy desk to call.[24]

During her first few years at *Vogue* she wrote merchandising and promotional copy. Her editor, Allene Talmey, probably contributed to the spare leanness of Didion's style, for she believed in drastic cutting, "writing long and publishing short."[25] By 1961 she was writing feature pieces for *Vogue* and doing an occasional article for the *National Review* as well as for *Mademoiselle*.

Despite the wonder that she felt at being in New York, Didion was often homesick; it was in part to deal with this feeling that she began to draft her first novel, *Run River*, set in the Sacramento Valley. Discovering immense satisfaction in the writing of fiction, she decided to go on leave from her full-time position at *Vogue* to devote more time to it (she continued as film critic for the magazine for several years, however). Published in the spring of 1963, *Run River* created barely a ripple in the literary world, receiving a handful of mixed reviews.

Of all that Didion loved about New York, only her work and a few close friends were substantial; pleasure in new people and places is by its nature ephemeral, for at some point they cease to be new. Because Didion came to the city to enlarge her experience rather than to find security, she never bothered to find a permanent residence. For much of the eight years she lived in other people's apartments; even when she rented her own, the only furniture she bought was a bed. For several years (we don't know the exact dates, but 1959–61 is a reasonable guess) she lived with another writer; she has written that, although she cried when she left him, he was unmoved.[26]

Didion gradually became disenchanted with her life in New York, and by 1963 disillusion had deepened into depression. Given to bouts of uncontrollable crying, she saw a doctor, who recommended a psychiatrist. She never saw the psychiatrist; instead she married, in January

1964, John Gregory Dunne, a writer at *Time* whom she had known for six years and lived with for one. Marriage did not lift her depression, however; she could not work, talk to people, or even "get dinner with any degree of certainty."[27] In response to her emotional paralysis Dunne took a leave of absence from *Time*, and they went to Los Angeles. Although they kept their apartment in New York for a year, they never returned there to live. "New York is . . . a city for only the very young," Didion wrote three years later, although in the same piece she conceded that, given the romantic illusions she brought with her, she might have had the same kind of experience in "Paris or Chicago or even San Francisco."[28]

Shortly after her marriage Didion had a miscarriage that she experienced as both physically and emotionally devastating.[29] Badly wanting a child, in 1966 she and Dunne adopted a baby girl whom they named Quintana Roo after a territory in the Yucatan. The child was (and is) a source of joy to Didion, who assumed primary responsibility for her care from the moment of her arrival.

Didion's marriage to Dunne has survived separation as well as emotional and economic stress. In the summer of 1968, his writing going badly, Dunne moved into a residential motel in Las Vegas; for the next eighteen months he spent more time there than in the house on Franklin Avenue in Los Angeles where Didion lived with their baby. In December 1969 Didion opened a column for *Life* with the acknowledgement that she was in Honolulu with her husband and daughter in lieu of filing for divorce; she blamed their problems on her emotional withdrawal rather than his separate residence, and closed the piece with her promise to him that she would try to "make things matter."[30]

When, in 1978, Didion looked back at the period between 1966 and 1971, she acknowledged that during this time she felt life to be meaningless, unintelligible. In 1966 an article on Hawaii that she wrote for *The Saturday Eve-*

ning Post opened with the confession that "Because I had been tired too long and quarrelsome too much and too often frightened of migraine and failure and the days getting shorter, I was sent, a recalcitrant thirty-one-year-old child, to Hawaii, where winter does not come and no one fails and the median age is twenty-three."[31] Although she functioned during this period as a writer, parent, hostess and citizen, she did not know why she was playing any of these roles; she felt that life's secret was locked in a trunk, the key long ago discarded.[32]

In fact Didion was suffering recurrent depression, sometimes mild and sometimes intense enough to produce nausea and dizziness.[33] The depression did not often impair her functioning, however, for she wrote productively between 1966 and 1971. She was published regularly in *The Saturday Evening Post* and occasionally in *Holiday*, *The American Scholar*, *The New York Times Magazine* and *National Review*. From 1967 until the *Post* ceased publication in 1969, she and Dunne alternated writing a column called "Points West," consisting of brief articles on persons and events in California. In 1968 she collected twenty articles written during the sixties and published them under the title of the piece on Haight-Ashbury, *Slouching Towards Bethlehem*. Her second novel, *Play It As It Lays*, published in 1970, became a best-seller and was nominated for a National Book Award. With Dunne, she wrote the screenplay for *Panic in Needle Park*, a film about young heroin addicts that received a prize at the Cannes Film Festival.

While her professional reputation soared, however, she privately felt a lack of direction and purpose to her life: "I was supposed to have a script, and had mislaid it. I was supposed to hear cues, and no longer did."[34] There were months when she couldn't work and other months when she worked despite constant emotional pain. She was deeply disturbed by the social dislocations of the sixties, but she assumed full personal responsibility for her own condition: "I . . . could lay off my own state of profound emotional shock on the larger cultural breakdown, could talk fast about convulsions in the society and alienation and anomie and maybe even assassination, but that would be just one more stylish shell game. I am not the society in microcosm. I am a thirty-four-year-old woman with long straight hair and an old bikini bathing suit and bad nerves . . ."[35] Ten years later she would postulate a closer connection between social and political events and her own feelings; in 1969 she still felt, as she had in college, that she should be able to reach "a separate peace."

After 1971 Didion's depression eased considerably. The critical and popular success of *Play It As It Lays* must have significantly allayed her fear of failure. Although she continued to do reporting, she chose quieter, less violent subjects. While in the late sixties she wrote pieces on convicted murderers (the Ferguson brothers) and drug-dazed children ("Slouching Towards Bethlehem"), in the seventies she wrote on the Getty Museum, the Governor's mansion, and the California waterworks. It may be the case that she lost her need to penetrate violent and disorderly modes of experience; or it may be simply that she perceived the seventies as a calm after the storms of Vietnam, Berkeley, and Kent State.

Her marriage also became steadier. In 1971 she and Dunne moved out of their rented house on Franklin Avenue into a beach house that they purchased in Trancas, forty miles north of Los Angeles on the Pacific Coast. The move itself suggests a quest for a quieter, more stable life. The house on Franklin Avenue stood in a part of Hollywood that had once been elegant, but in the sixties the large houses needed paint and other repairs, and the neighborhood "was peopled mainly by rock-and-roll bands, therapy groups, very old women wheeled down the street by practical nurses in soiled uniforms, and by my husband, my daughter, and me."[36]

In Trancas, by contrast, Didion and Dunne found a

coherent community of neighbors who looked out for each other's children and property and stood ready to help against threats of fire, floods, and high winds. They invested a good deal of time, money, and energy in the house itself; elaborately constructed bookcases in the library took two months to build, and terra cotta tile floors took six months to lay. With a wide terrace overhanging the Pacific and high redwood ceilings in every room, the result of their efforts was stunning in its openness and simplicity. Even more significant, the house expressed a stable marriage and a firmly rooted past; its furnishings included a rosewood piano that had sailed around the Cape to Didion's family in 1848, a hanging quilt made by her great-great grandmother on a wagon train, and a Federal table that had belonged to Dunne's great-grandmother.[37]

The seven years that they spent in Trancas were productive for both Didion and Dunne. Working in a small room in the guesthouse (without a telephone), Didion wrote her most ambitious novel, *A Book of Common Prayer*, an immediate best-seller in 1977. She also wrote articles for *Esquire*, *The Los Angeles Times Book Review*, *The New York Times Book Review*, *The New York Review of Books*, and *New West*. Dunne wrote *True Confessions* during this period; it was to become his first best-seller. They worked together on several screenplays, including one for the film version of *Play It As It Lays*.

Since their marriage, Didion and Dunne have edited each other's work. Asked about this aspect of their relationship, Didion answered, " . . . it works out very well. We trust each other. . . . there is a tacit understanding that neither of us will push too far."[38] Although rumors of marital difficulties surface from time to time, their own statements—and they are painfully honest—testify to a mutually supportive relationship. When Susan Braudy from *Ms.* asked Didion in 1977 why, as a superbly functioning woman herself, she didn't create strong women in her novels, Dunne broke the ensuing silence by asserting,

"Whoever asks that question doesn't know a damn thing about the questions of literature. Joan writes because she writes."[39]

Life in Trancas posed problems they had not anticipated, however. Rattlesnakes in the driveway were not uncommon; at times fires or floods extensive enough to close the highway occurred. In their last year there, the floods were so heavy that the highway collapsed, and one of Quintana's friends drowned at Zuma Beach. Didion began to have fantasies about "a house with a center-hall plan with the living room on your right and the dining hall on your left."[40] In the summer of 1978 they bought such a house, a two-story colonial on Chadbourne Avenue in Brentwood Park, a well-kept but unpretentious section of Los Angeles. A few months after they moved, a fire that had started in the San Fernando Valley and been carried to the Pacific Coast by high winds destroyed 197 houses, including many belonging to their friends in Trancas; the fire had stopped a mere 125 feet from the property they had just sold.[41]

In June 1979 Simon and Schuster released *The White Album*, a collection of essays written between 1968 and 1978. At the beginning of the book Didion copied verbatim a psychiatric report of her condition based on tests she took in an outpatient clinic in Santa Monica in the summer of 1968. The report referred to her "fundamentally pessimistic and oppressive view of the world around her" and her feeling that "she lives in a world of people moved by strange, conflicted, poorly comprehended, and, above all, devious motivations which commit them inevitably to conflict and failure."[42] It claimed that her personality was in the process of deteriorating and that her ego was unable to mediate the world of reality.

Didion's inclusion of the report was a bold stroke, for it was presumably an "objective" view of her, and it invited us to think of her as crazy. The next fifteen brief essays describe with factual objectivity events that occurred between 1966 and 1971; Didion was either actually present at most of the events or interviewed some of the principals involved. The events include the assassination of Robert Kennedy; riots at San Francisco State College; the attempt of Black Panthers to make a hero of Huey Newton, arrested on charges of murdering a white police officer; and the Manson murders. One of the most telling essays describes a recording session of a rock group at which no recording took place since the musicians failed even to acknowledge each other's presence in the room. (The group was the Doors, whose music insisted that love was sex and sex was death.) By the time we finish the fifteen essays, we feel that Didion's emotional state was not madness but the appropriate response of a sensitive woman to a chaos she personally witnessed. She no longer believed, as she did in 1969, that she could live outside of history, relatively untouched by public and political events. Writing in 1978 she offered this pungent comment on the psychiatric report: " . . . an attack of vertigo and nausea does not now seem to me an inappropriate response to the summer of 1968."[43]

While Didion looked back upon the sixties as a nightmarish time of chaos, she viewed the seventies as more orderly. She was still concerned to unmask its folly and pretension, but, because its events were intelligible, they were less overwhelming and more susceptible to analysis.

The White Album was nationally acclaimed for the depth of its insight into the sixties and early seventies in the United States as well as for its precision and economy of style. Interviewed in the spring of 1979 just before its appearance, Didion appeared relaxed, even cheerful. Although she conceded that the white stucco house with the center-hall plan did not remove the risk from life, as it had in her fantasy, there is a playful note to the interview, and her present life seems productive and orderly. Currently working on a new novel (tentatively entitled *Angel*

Visits), she pursues a disciplined schedule that calls for her to write from eleven until four or five, when she makes herself a drink and edits her day's work. She achieves order through smaller rituals, too—making curtains, polishing the silver, cooking dinner each night. In her own life, as in the lives of her fictional characters, these daily tasks serve the purposes that religious rituals once did; they help to ward off evil and to render everyday life intelligible.[44]

Asked about religion in a 1977 interview, Didion replied that she was raised an Episcopalian but had stopped going to church because she could not understand the parables: "But I am quite religious in a certain way . . . I like the words of the Episcopal service, and I say them over and over in my mind."[45] Didion is religious "in a certain way"; she believes that there may be forces beyond man and nature, and that prayer, whether or not it influences these forces, has for some people the power to soothe pain and mitigate grief.

Didion disliked the Biblical parables because they often offended her moral sense: "I have never understood why the prodigal son should be treated any better than the other son."[46] While not conventionally religious, she is a stern moralist for whom right and wrong are powerful realities. Her moral sense pervades both her fiction, which dramatizes moral issues, and her essays, which analyze them. The basis of her morality is not an ideology, however, but a broad and compassionate humanism; she believes that social ideology leads to "the coarsening of moral imagination," and affirms that her own writing is committed to "the exploration of moral distinctions and ambiguities."[47]

Didion thinks of herself as a writer, a "person whose most absorbed and passionate hours are spent arranging words on pieces of paper."[48] She does not think of herself as a teacher, although she spent a semester as a visiting regents lecturer at Berkeley in 1975; she does not think of herself as an intellectual (in her definition, a person who deals with abstractions), although most of her readers doubtless do. Writing is for her an act of self-discovery: "I write entirely to find out what I'm thinking, what I'm looking at, what I see and what it means. What I want and what I fear."[49] She wrote before she could articulate her reasons for writing; as a pre-adolescent whose short life had been fragmented by the war, she wrote stories the very immaturity of which was an attempt to discover and shape strong feeling into a form that could control and order it. The following incident, recounted in a 1977 interview, reveals the extent to which writing is for Didion the means and the symbol of the coherent self:

I remember one day we had a bunch of people here for a beach party, and the house was filled with people. I began to feel scattered, upset, not myself . . . I went to my office and just sat in front of my typewriter, and it was okay. I got control. I calmed down. I'm only myself in front of my typewriter.[50]

Didion's view of herself as a writer explains much, including the stark honesty with which she reveals herself in her essays. Her fiction and essays are formed of much more than deep personal need, however. They do reflect this, but they reflect also her extensive reading in American and European literature, her experience as an American and a Californian, and her knowledge of particular American subcultures. From her felt private need Didion has created novels of brilliant formal and thematic integrity; the chapters that follow will analyze the forms and themes of this fiction, beginning with her most celebrated novel, *Play It As It Lays*.

2

Play It As It Lays

After World War I American novelists chronicled the impact of war and industrialization on a generation taught to respect the traditional institutions of religion, marriage, and democracy. The heroes of Hemingway and Fitzgerald cannot find their salvation in these institutions; they either develop a personal moral code, or they become members of what Gertrude Stein termed "the lost generation." Although the generation of the twenties could not believe deeply in God, family or country, however, these institutions nevertheless served to provide ideals that everyone recognized, a heritage against which rebellion and skepticism might be measured. The Hemingway hero might not be able to pray, but he has a highly developed moral sense; he has rejected the ritual of religion, but the concepts of sacrifice, courage, and discipline still have meaning for him.

The American novelist of the sixties and seventies is writing of a later generation, one that is "lost" in a different and deeper sense. The contemporary individual is unlikely to have a patriotic or religious heritage; he must live in a society whose materialistic and pleasure-seeking values lack the moral dimension provided by traditional institutions. Although the moral vision of early twentieth-century America—of a world "safe for democracy," and for women and children as well—may have been betrayed by the realities of war and capitalism, contemporary

society has no shared moral vision at all, and the person
with a private moral vision requires tremendous energy
and courage to live by it or even to articulate it. The
novelist who portrays such an individual inevitably
stresses his loneliness, for the people around him in all
likelihood do not even understand, much less support, his
values. One thinks, for example, of Morris Bober, the
poor Jewish shopkeeper in Bernard Malamud's *The
Assistant*. Bober is isolated because his materialistic
neighbors—and even his wife—think of him as a failed
man whose readiness to trust a stranger and extend credit
to a hungry drunk is stupid. The isolation of the individual and the moral chaos of a competitive society are
the special province of the contemporary novelist.

Maria Wyeth, the central character of Didion's *Play
It As It Lays*, is the contemporary heroine *par excellence*, for
she nurtures a secret dream of family solidarity while living and working in Hollywood and Beverly Hills, among
people who recognize only power, success, and physical
beauty and pleasure. At the age of eighteen Maria left her
home in Silver Wells, Nevada, at her father's urging, to
take acting lessons in New York. Her father saw no conflict between the values of family closeness and his
daughter's potential career as an actress; aware of her
beauty, he sent her forth with the assurance that "You're
holding all the aces, baby."

With no exposure to religion or humanistic education, Maria's entire philosophy consists of two maxims
taught her by her father. The first is that life is a crap
game to be played like a craps layout—as it lies. He wants
her to play the game in New York, where the stakes are
high, and where her beauty and talent will be the "aces"
that she plays to win. Harry Wyeth's philosophy is a
perversion of the religious belief of early Americans that,
because of their essential innocence, they were objects of
God's special grace, grace enabling the individual to confront and conquer his destiny. In Wyeth's version of this

belief God is absent, and the optimism inherent in the belief is tied to games of chance rather than the benevolent power of a deity. But Wyeth's blind trust in the future, his conviction that anyone with talent and ambition must be fortunate, is a variation on the dream that F. Scott Fitzgerald embodied in the "great" Gatsby. "I was raised to believe," Maria tells the reader, "that what came in on the next roll would always be better than what went out on the last." The belief is a trivial secularization of the positive side of the original American dream: the sense of God's special covenant with Americans.

The early American view of God's special care of our country existed in tension with a sense of ever-present evil to be perpetually guarded against. The second lesson that Wyeth teaches his daughter, that anyone who overturns a rock is "apt to reveal a rattlesnake," is a secularization of the dark side of the American religious heritage, the Calvinistic sense of lurking evil. As the form assumed by Satan to seduce Eve, the snake is one of our oldest symbols of evil—and the rattlesnake is a peculiarly American snake. Ironically, the symbol of evil in Wyeth's philosophy is far more concrete and tangible than his symbol of good, which is luck in a game of chance.

In eighteenth and nineteenth-century America both the sense of God's special grace and that of Satan's dangerous power were part of a traditional faith that sustained both individuals and communities, a moral vision whose center was man, pulled between the poles of God and Satan. The vision explained both good and evil and offered man consolation for earthly suffering in its possibility of eternal salvation. Drained of this comprehensive moral vision, Wyeth's lessons hardly provide a viable philosophy. They acknowledge that both good and evil exist in the world, but they conceive of good as material success and of evil as a fact of nature. Furthermore, they are not entirely consistent: the first maxim, play it as it lays, counsels Maria to be an opportunist; the second, beware of the rattlesnake beneath every rock, counsels fear and passivity. What the two maxims do have in common is the suggestion that one who is passive and clever can win what he wants without sustained effort. They also hint that one should not look beneath the surface of a situation; opportunities can be seized only if one accepts them at face value, without attempting to alter or analyze them.

Maria accepts her father's maxims, as well as his ambition for her, without question. She fails to see the conflict between the two maxims, or even that between her father's ambition for her and his professed concern for her well-being. Because of her passivity and lack of reflective analysis, as well as the selfishness of the people around her, she becomes the exploited rather than the exploiter. The attempt to live by her father's morally bankrupt philosophy brings her ultimately to the exclusive Los Angeles psychiatric institution from which she makes the opening statement of the novel.

In this statement Maria speaks directly to the reader as she looks back over her life—her childhood in Silver Wells, her career as a successful model in New York City, her marriage to (and subsequent estrangement from) movie director Carter Lang. Her thoughts are interlaced with two images from her father's maxims, one of a poisonous snake (which represents evil and death) and the other of a card game (which, like the image of a crap game, represents life). Her monologue concludes with the question, "Maybe I was holding all the aces, but what was the game?" Two brief fragments follow this introduction—one the voice of Helene, her former friend, and the other that of Carter, her former husband: feeling themselves rejected by Maria, neither can empathize with her pain.

The novel itself, narrated in the third person, is the chronicle of Maria Wyeth's emotional breakdown. Its time frame is approximately one year, and its structure consists of brief chapters (the shortest is fifty words) describing incidents that deepen her depression. The principal setting is Beverly Hills, and the persons surrounding Maria are actors, producers, agents, and directors, most of whom are cold, manipulative, and exploitative. Having walked off the set of her latest picture, Maria has not worked for nearly a year; she fills her empty life with visits to her brain-damaged daughter, Kate, who is permanently hospitalized, and with long drives on the freeway, drives leading nowhere. Her worst fear is realized when she discovers that she is pregnant and does not know whether Carter or her lover, Les Goodwin, is the father. Carter insists that she have an abortion, and Maria, who exercises a rapidly dwindling control over her own life, yields to his demand. Her illegal abortion becomes the central event of the novel, both literally, because she cannot recover from the loss and guilt it produces, and figuratively, because all relationships in the novel are aborted—sometimes by Maria herself, but more often by the cruelty or indifference of others.

Although many people claim concern for Maria, they fail to give her sustained support or real understanding; they can only suggest that she get out to more parties. Toward the conclusion of the novel Carter, alarmed by her withdrawal, invites her to come to the desert on location with him. Their attempt at reunion fails, however, for when he finds Maria sexually unresponsive, Carter treats her alternately like a bitch and a child. The person who understands Maria best is Carter's producer BZ; like her, he is disgusted by the decadence that enmeshes them. Unlike her, however, he decides to withdraw from the game altogether; one night when they are alone, he takes a deliberate overdose of Seconal and dies in her arms. It is after this incident that we find Maria in a psychiatric institution, fantasizing about a future in which she lives alone with her daughter Kate, engaged in the simple pastoral activity of preserving fruit.

Play It As It Lays is a grim portrayal of a world in which people use each other to gain success, recognition, or sensual pleasure. Among Maria's friends and lovers no relationship is too sacred to be exploited. Carter himself objectifies Maria in two movies: in the first he shoots scenes of her daily life without telling her of his intention to tie them together in a film ("At the end she was thrown into negative and looked dead."); in the second, a commercial film, she plays a luckless girl raped by an entire motorcycle gang.[1] As a rich producer, BZ has considerable influence with young actresses; when his friend Larry Kulik mentions his desire to "get into" a particular "young girl in a white halter dress," BZ arranges for the satisfaction of Larry's desire. BZ's wife Helene is paid large sums by her mother-in-law to stay married, presumably because the marriage serves to disguise (albeit thinly) BZ's homosexuality.

In the culture of Beverly Hills sexual activity, in addition to a means of sensual pleasure, is a defense against boredom and a mode of hostility. The one sexual encounter described in detail in the novel is between Maria and an actor she meets at a party:

When they finally did it they were on the bed and at the moment before he came he reached under the pillow and pulled out an amyl nitrate popper and broke it under his nose, breathed in rapidly, and closed his eyes.

"Don't move," he said. *"I said don't move."*

Maria did not move.

"Terrific," he said then. His eyes were still closed.

Maria said nothing.

"Wake me up in three hours," he said. "With your tongue."

The actor commands Maria to behave in the way that will most enhance his pleasure; he has not the least concern for hers. So impersonal is the encounter, in fact, that he does not bother to look at her when it is over.

The element of affection is absent from all sexual activity, its place filled with drink, drugs, or violence. When

Maria gets drunk at a party, Helene and BZ take her to their house, undress her, and use her as both a stimulus to and a participant in their sadomasochistic play. Didion does not describe the orgy itself, but rather concentrates on the reactions of the participants the next morning. Maria remembers BZ holding a belt and Helene laughing; Helene, her face puffy and bruised, now cries. BZ will not permit either of them to express regret: "If you can't deal with the morning, get out of the game. You've been around a long time, you know what it is, it's play-or-pay." BZ, too, lives within the metaphor of life as a game of dice or cards; as in craps or poker, if a player is behind, he must either keep playing or pay his way out of the game.

Although the private lives of these people are not attractive, they expend much money and effort to maintain external beauty and the appearance of youth. Even in the depths of her depression, Maria remembers to eat her hard-boiled-egg lunch without salt, since salt can bloat, and BZ is described as "perpetually tanned, oiled, gleaming . . . tanned as evidence of a lifetime spent in season." The fear of ugliness cuts incredibly deep; when Helene's hairdresser is out of town, she confides to Maria, "If I'm *in* town, and Leonard's *not*, I feel almost . . . frightened." The illusion of youth is demanded, as is the "correct" style in dress, food, even drink. And this style is modish, even precious. It is important to BZ's lover that drinks be mixed with real rather than reconstituted lemons; it is important to Maria's escorts that she "could always distinguish among the right bracelet and the amusing impersonation of the right bracelet and the bracelet that was merely a witless copy."

Both men and women in this culture are perceived as decorative and sexual objects; no one is valued for himself. Persons with money and power are respected for their success, however, and, since most of the people with economic power are men, women are at a perpetual

disadvantage unless they are protected by a powerful
man. All of Maria's casual acquaintances view her as
Carter's property. When she meets an actor in an
elevator, "the look he gave . . . was dutifully charged
with sexual appreciation, not for Maria herself but for
Carter Lang's wife." When Maria expresses anger to
Johnny Waters, who reported her for stealing his car,
Waters responds, "Just hold on, cunt. . . . *You never told
me who you were.*" Although the police find marijuana in
Waters' car when they stop Maria in it, Carter's agent arranges to have the discovery of the drug removed from the
report, for even the law respects those who have money
and power.

Maria cannot survive among these "beautiful people"
because her private dream is completely at odds with their
values, and she lacks the courage and discipline to live out
the dream alone. Central to Maria's dream, and foremost
in her value system, is the traditional concept of the
family—a group that includes mother, father, and child,
and within which people work and love. In her favorite
fantasy, which also occurs as a dream, she lives with her
lover Les Goodwin and her daughter Kate in a house by
the sea:

Every morning in that house she would make the bed with fresh
sheets. Every day in that house she would cook while Kate did
her lessons. Kate would sit in a shaft of sunlight, her head bent
over a pine table, and later when the tide ran out they would
gather mussels together, Kate and Maria, and still later all three
of them would sit down together at the big pine table and Maria
would light a kerosene lamp and they would eat the mussels and
drink a bottle of cold white wine . . .

In the real world, however, Goodwin is married to someone else, Kate will never do lessons, and the mussels on
the California shore are toxic.

Maria's vision of the family is an idealization of her
own family life as an only child. She has nostalgic

memories both of her childhood relationships with her now-dead parents and of visits with them after she had moved to New York. In one remembered scene Maria is eating dinner with her parents (spareribs rather than mussels, but cooked by her mother) when she announces that she does not want to go back to the city. Her mother would like her to stay, but her father is ambitious for her: "She can't win if she's not at the table, Francine." When Francine Wyeth is killed in a car accident soon after this visit, Maria is unable to work for a month, for not only was she devoted to her mother, but her mother's death (her body was devoured by coyotes before it was found) also seems confirmation of the evil in the world, the rattlesnake under the rock.

Although far from ideal, Maria's family was a unit, and its members were bound by affection for each other. (When her mother dies, her father writes her, "Honey, this is a bad hand if there ever was one, but God never meant it to set you back in your plans.") Maria remembers her mother, in particular, with guilt and love, for the bond between mother and child is her highest value, a value communicated to the reader but not to her friends and not even to the psychiatrists in the hospital, who are more concerned to know whether she sees "a cock in this inkblot." The chain of love in the novel passes from Francine to Maria to Kate and is shown in gestures more than words; Maria remembers her mother cutting her hair in bangs, and when she visits her hospitalized daughter she brushes Kate's hair, working out "the tangles into fine golden strands." At the close of the novel Maria's single ambition is to get Kate out of the hospital and live with her, but her wish is an unrealistic one in view of both her own weakness and her child's condition.

Maria has the opportunity to bear a healthy child when she becomes pregnant early in the novel, but Carter insists that she have an abortion, and she is too guilty about the pregnancy, the result of her affair with Les

Goodwin, to resist. After the abortion Maria realizes that the child she and Les conceived was the essence of their relationship, and she no longer derives pleasure from their clandestine meetings. The reader mourns the loss with Maria, wishing that she had been strong enough to bear and raise the child alone. But there are no children in the novel, and Maria's parental and filial love are frustrated by both private tragedy and the failure of her culture to either acknowledge or support such love.

Like her friends, Maria has the discipline required to work (she acts in a television production even when bleeding heavily from the abortion) but not the discipline or energy required to maintain closeness in an adult relationship. When Maria tells Carter that she is pregnant by Les,

She wanted to tell him she was sorry, but saying she was sorry did not seem entirely adequate, and in any case what she was sorry about seemed at once too deep and too evanescent for any words she knew, seemed so vastly more complicated than the immediate fact that it was perhaps better left unraveled.

On the one occasion when Maria tells Carter she loves him, he seems not to hear. It is ironic that among these aggressive and sexually active people, real love and real remorse must be suppressed. Even ordinary kindness is suspected; when Maria meets an unbalanced woman in a coffee shop and responds to the woman's expression of loneliness by touching her in reassurance, the woman screams and orders her to remove her "whore's hands."

Although Maria does not share the hollow values of the jet set, she shares many of their limitations. In particular, she shares with them an aversion to analysis and reflection, a tendency to experience life in terms of scenes remembered or imagined rather than in logical terms of cause and effect. Maria does not reflect that her relationship with Ivan Costello ended because he screamed at her and drank too much; instead she remembers "the exact way the light came through the shutters in his bedroom in

New York, the exact colors of the striped sheets she had put on his bed." She does not understand the role that her own depression played in the failure of her marriage to Carter, but she remembers scenes from her life with him: "Kate fevered, Carter sponging her back while Maria called the pediatrician. Kate's birthday, Kate laughing, Carter blowing out the candle." It is as if Maria has in some perverse way been affected by her professional role as model and actress; she views her life not as a coherent pattern susceptible to rational understanding but as a series of images flashed on a screen.

In the first-person statement that opens the novel Maria announces her refusal to seek reasons for anything, but she never understands that without reasoned insight she will not be able to control her life. If life is a game of craps, of course, then not only is control impossible, but decision, discipline, and will have no meaningful role to play. In the entire novel Maria makes few positive decisions, and she demonstrates her will primarily in refusing to go to parties. She does makes a series of negative resolutions, a list of things she will never do, but by the conclusion of the novel, she has broken several of the promises to herself: "She would never: *ball at a party, do S-M unless she wanted to, borrow furs from Abe Lipsey, deal.*" Like most of Maria's behavior, the list is impulsive; it represents a bizarre mixture of moral resolutions with matters of taste and has little weight because not rationally designed to begin with.

Ironically, Maria would very much like to control her life; part of her fascination with the film that she made with Carter derives from the "knack" for control that the girl demonstrates. But she has no understanding of the processes of planning and following through which give people a measure of control over their destinies. Instead, she seeks control through magic and ritual. Fearing that she is pregnant in the early chapters of the novel, she tries to induce her period through a series of actions designed to show the fates that she does not expect it: "To be without Tampax was to insure bleeding, to sleep naked between white sheets was to guarantee staining. . . . She wore white crepe pajamas and no underwear to a party." She has accepted not only her father's view of life as a game of chance, but the superstitions associated with such games, the notion that Lady Luck can be summoned, appeased, even tricked.

Maria believes that sin and guilt lead inevitably to punishment; this connection is in fact the one cause-and-effect relationship that she consistently perceives. She expects to die from the abortion "as unquestionably as she believed that loveless marriage ended in cancer of the cervix and equivocal adultery in fatal accidents to children." But if life is a game of chance, it cannot also be a logical matter of cause and effect: whence the inconsistency in Maria's attitudes? From two sources, I think. Didion believes that women predictably feel . guilty after an abortion because they are natural bearers of children, mysteriously involved with "blood and birth and death."[2] She also regards Maria's guiltiness (which is invariably associated with sexual activity) as the result of social conditioning, the burden of her generation of women.

Maria survives the abortion, of course, but her expectation of punishment continues. When she receives in the mail an advertisement from a hypnotist stating that "Your worries may date from when you were a baby in your mother's womb," she calls to make an appointment with him despite a terrible fear that she will learn some ominous fact about her conception or infancy. Ironically, her problems do in part date from her childhood, but their causes are cultural and psychological; they do not spring from a single terrifying fact, "the rattlesnake under the rock."

Maria feels that if she can regress to infancy in a hypnotic trance, she may learn a truth that, although terrible, will help her to understand and control her life. Her sessions with the hypnotist prove to be a meaningless exercise, however, for he blames his failure to put Maria in a trance on her resistance, her fear of the truth.

Maria turns to magic and ritual much as Hemingway's heroes turn to religion, as a last resort, with a desperate hope that they may ward off disaster. Whereas Hemingway's priests are dignified and generous, however, even when they cannot convert the hero, Didion's hypnotist is neither. Always shivering with cold, he continuously drinks Pernod and water. The hypnotist and his house are both shabby, and the implications of his advertisement are false, for he cannot deliver the insight he offers. He has not the passion for hypnosis that Hemingway's priests have for God; in fact his only motive is a commercial one. Thus the figure of the hypnotist in the novel is one more illustration of the spiritual poverty of contemporary life.

Perhaps Maria's dream of a close family leading a simple life could not be realized in contemporary America, even were she capable of discipline and rational analysis; without these qualities the dream is clearly impossible. Maria does not relinquish the dream, however; she clings to it even after her breakdown, but it becomes progressively more divorced from the realities of her life. Maria's relationship with the society that surrounds her is a complex one, because she is both a victim of its values and a cause of her own undoing. Only by looking closely at the fragmented action of the novel can one precisely understand this relationship.

Throughout the novel, Maria lives alone. She cannot even say clearly whether Carter left her or she left him; their marriage simply collapsed under the weight of her sorrow over Kate, his compulsive working, and their joint failure to communicate their feelings. Maria deals with her fear and loneliness by spending the day driving on the

highways of Los Angeles; her driving seems pointless, a
distraction, an end in itself, until, at the end of chapter 6,
we realize that through her long drives she is moving
toward Carter, on location in the desert. Finding herself
only 60 miles from him, she would like to call, but the
conversations she remembers led only to rage on both
sides, and, afraid of rage, afraid of rejection, she does not
call. The drives toward the desert are the first instance of
a pattern that dominates Maria's relationships with all the
people in her life. The pattern is an elaborate dance: when
the partner moves towards her, she moves away; when he
moves away, she follows. The dance enables Maria to
avoid emotional closeness and the mutual responsibility it
implies; it also serves her need for suffering and self-
punishment, since it keeps her alone and isolated. She
doesn't tell Les Goodwin that she is pregnant, even
though he is probably the father of the child; she ignores
his messages for days, then calls him impulsively from a
pay phone. Although she feels "a rush of well-being" when
she hears his voice, she says only "call me" before hanging
up. At dinner with him on the evening of the day of the
abortion she asserts her wish to go somewhere that music
is played loudly; the reason she gives is that she is tired of
listening to "them all," but the deeper reason is that she
doesn't want to share her pain and loneliness.

Part of Maria's technique for ensuring that she does
not get the help she needs is to ask help only of people who
can't or won't give it. Both Carter and Goodwin seem gen-
uinely concerned for her, but when Maria is frightened
after the failure of her sessions with the hypnotist she
turns, not to either of them, but to Ivan Costello, whom
she dislikes. Drunk and angry, he responds by spitting at
her over the phone. Apparently sorry the next morning,
he leaves four messages for her on the service, but she
returns none of them. When Maria runs into Benny
Austin, her parents' old friend, at the Flamingo, she is
threatened by his talk of the past and pleads fatigue in
order to get away from him. Simultaneously attracted to

and repelled by her past, however, a few weeks later she drives to Las Vegas and tries to find him. Finding that his phone is no longer in service, she waits three days in the post office for him to get his mail from his box. When the box is finally opened, however, it is by a woman with a "hard sad face" who has never heard of Benny Austin and views Maria with suspicion. Maria stays in Vegas, wandering in and out of hotels, coming precariously close to breaking her resolution never to walk through the Sands after midnight. By the end of a week there she is on the verge of a breakdown, doubting the solidity and reality of her own body, "thinking constantly about where her body stopped and the air began, about the exact point in space and time that was the difference between Maria and *other*." At the end of two weeks she runs into her agent, who tells her that her isolation isn't healthy and invites her to a party; it is a measure of the sickness of Maria's society that her friends think that her emotional illness can be eased through drinking, sex, and small talk.

The most elaborate steps in this dance of ambivalence are those Maria takes with Carter. She wants to move Carter to feel and act on her behalf, but she does not feel for him; she wants him to respond sexually to her, although she does not respond sexually to him. When she knows definitely that she is pregnant she gives the entire problem, including her uncertainty about the father, to him; his response is first to feel helpless ("What in fuck am I supposed to do?") and then to find a doctor who will do a "clean" abortion for her (abortion was still illegal in California in the sixties). He persuades her to have the abortion with a threat to take custody of Kate if she doesn't, although it isn't clear how he could have done this, and Maria really offers little resistance.

About divorce they are both ambivalent; the dance goes on in their conversation:

"I'm going to do it," she would say on the telephone.
"Then do it," Carter would say. "It's better."

"You think it's better."
"If it's what you want."
"What do *you* want."

A few months after the abortion they actually divorce, a legal procedure that is staged very much like a scene in a film, with Maria claiming mental cruelty and Helene confirming that Carter had repeatedly struck and humiliated his wife. If the charges are unreal, however, the loss of the relationship is real, and part of Maria's pain derives from the fact that no one around her acknowledges the end of the marriage with sympathy or sadness. Divorce is the norm in Maria's set, and scarcely even interesting. Helene pays more attention to the lesbian actresses lunching in the Bistro on the day of the hearing than she does to Maria, whom she scolds: "You look like hell, Maria, this isn't any excuse for you to fall apart, I mean a *divorce*."

Love and the commitment to another that it implies are not only dangerous, but also unfashionable. By the closing chapters of the novel, when Carter and Maria are together in the motel on the desert, they are not even tempted by love or sex, although they are sufficiently involved to continue the dance:

"What's the matter," Maria said, standing in the doorway in the dark.
"It isn't any better."
"How do you know."
He said nothing.
"I mean we didn't even try."
"You don't want it."
"I do too."
"No," he said. "You don't."

Carter still cares enough to curse her passivity, and Maria cares enough to ask him coldly if he enjoyed sex with Susannah, but their mutual anger now seems to be the only bond between them.

Maria has no close women friends. Her closest friend

is BZ, and the bond between them is their vulnerability. More deeply depressed even than Maria, BZ pretends that he doesn't care at all, when in fact he cares too much. When Helene and Carter begin an affair, BZ invites Maria to join him in suicide. She refuses, but is not able to dissuade him from taking an overdose of Seconal. He warns her, "Some day you'll wake up and you just won't feel like playing any more." But even on the edge of madness, Maria has at her core a toughness that makes her a survivor. In the final chapter of the novel she tells the reader that she is still in the game of life, although she cannot give a reason to be—"I know what 'nothing' means and keep on playing." Maria is still playing, but her only game now is solitaire ("Now I lie in the sun and play solitaire and listen to the sea . . ."). She never understands that the game she was playing was in fact the child's game of hide-and-seek—the real Maria hid behind a wall of indifference, half wanting and half afraid of discovery.

Maria's game of hide-and-seek, in which she alternately approaches and withdraws from other characters, gives innumerable jagged turns to the action of the novel. The novel's coherence, then, springs not from its fragmented plot, but from its relentless focus on the character of Maria. After the three opening statements, the narrator never leaves Maria; although most of the narration is in the third person, it closely follows Maria's thoughts, dreams, memories, and behavior. Given this focus, we must ask why Didion included the brief statements by Helene and Carter at the beginning. It is significant that Didion has these two characters speak directly to the reader and directly about Maria. Both seem to be saying that they understand Maria, when in fact they conclude by dismissing her. Helene's approach is judgmental; she calls Maria careless and selfish and blames her for BZ's death. Although it would be hard to imagine a woman more selfish than Helene herself, there is a sense in which Helene speaks the truth; Maria could have made a more strenuous effort to save BZ than she did. The problem with Helene's approach, however, is that it sheds no light on Maria; it fails to explain her feelings or behavior.

Carter's approach to Maria is cinematic rather than judgmental. He begins, "Here are some scenes I have very clear in my mind," and proceeds to describe two scenes, one in which Maria cries after a trivial argument at a dinner party, and another in which Maria becomes annoyed with him for warning her not to let the baby (Kate) get chilled playing with the hose. Carter says that he has "played and replayed these scenes and others like them, composed them as if for the camera, trying to find some order, a pattern. I found none." However long and hard he observes her, Carter cannot understand Maria, for to understand her one must attend carefully to her thoughts, feelings, and memories. Carter's vision is that of the movie camera, which can record anger or depression, but has fewer resources than the novel to show the complex reasons for these feelings.

Didion may be saying that in certain cases the novel can explain and penetrate character more fully than the film can. This comparison seems to be suggested by Maria's own attitudes toward the films she made with Carter. In the first of these Carter simply followed her around and shot film of her doing ordinary things—sleeping on a couch at a party, doing a fashion sitting, crying on the IRT subway. Although the film, called simply *Maria*, won prizes at an Eastern European film festival, Maria hates it because "the girl on the screen . . . had no knack for anything." On the other hand, Maria likes *Angel Beach*, the commercial film she made with Carter, because the girl in that film takes command of her life at the end. In the case of this film, however, Maria has no feeling that the girl on the screen is herself. In describing Maria's thoughts about these films Didion seems to be asking, "Who is the real Maria, and how can she best be represented?" In fact the novel renders her with more insight and precision than the film that bears her name, because of the ease with which feelings and thoughts are presented in the novel form.

The film version of *Play It As It Lays*, although Didion and her husband John Dunne did the screenplay, was considered by reviewers to be false to the novel precisely because it did *not* focus on Maria's thoughts and feelings:

We never have much time to get inside Maria's mind because we're so busy reacting in our own ways to . . . the heated swimming pool unswum in, to the magnificent desert sunsets and sunrises unnoticed, to the glamorous parties that are supposed to be boring. . . .

Going to pieces this way doesn't seem all that terrifying, just extravagant.[3]

While acknowledging that Tuesday Weld as Maria and Anthony Perkins as BZ gave superior performances, Vincent Canby felt that, "unlike the novel, which evokes pity, the film is more likely to evoke . . . envy."[4] Because it is fundamentally a dramatic form, which portrays people from the outside, the film was unable to present the inner fantasies and terrors that define Maria's character.

In the novel, Didion manipulates point of view to bring the reader uncomfortably close to Maria's relentless sense of nothingness. So unobtrusive is the narrator throughout the central portions of the book that the reader scarcely notices when Didion begins to insert chapters spoken by Maria in the first person. In the last ten chapters the first-person point of view alternates with third-person narration. First Maria speaks from the hospital to which she has been committed; then Didion describes the events that lead up to BZ's suicide and her hospitalization. The alternation connects the immediate past with the present and also serves to close the circle of the plot. In the opening statement Maria claims that "nothing applies," that her life yields up no discernible pattern; in the closing chapter she announces that she has survived her confrontation with the meaninglessness of life:

. . . I know something Carter never knew, or Helene, or maybe you. I know what "nothing" means and keep on playing.
   Why, BZ would say.
   Why not, I say.

Didion creates in this passage—and the chapters that lead up to it—an intimacy between Maria and the reader that the medium of film could not duplicate. The intimacy is a source of terror, for when Maria compares her knowledge to ours we become aware of the latent possibility that we too might someday experience this essential void of meaning, the "nothingness" of experience.

We might—but Didion is not saying that we must. Maria and BZ see life as a hollow game of chance, but Didion does not see this metaphor as sufficient to encompass all the dimensions of life. Integrated into the novel is a figurative scheme that both challenges and supersedes the image of life as a crap game. The scheme uses traditional symbols: water as a symbol of spiritual renewal and the desert as the symbol of spiritual desolation. Only by recognizing these symbols can the reader combat the terror of "nothingness" that Maria's experience produces.

The symbols are easy to overlook because they are also part of the actual setting of the novel. The climactic action takes place on the Mojave desert, a place of moral desolation where all the characters act their worse. On the Mojave Desert Carter and Maria fight every night, Carter's leading actor physically abuses his leading actress in a drunken orgy, and BZ dies in Maria's bed. Didion refers again and again to the "motel on the desert" where Carter is filming; she also locates the town in which the motel is situated "on a dry river bed between Death Valley and the Nevada line." The barrenness and intense heat of the desert are both real conditions that irritate and depress

the characters and symbols of their despair and moral
sterility.

Significantly, Maria is the one person who has no
role in the filming, the one person who does not belong on
the desert. Her real affinity is for water: on her Beverly
Hills property she seems to spend all her time by the pool,
even sleeping next to it; in the hospital we see her in the
same proximity to water ("This morning I threw the coins
in the swimming pool and they turned and gleamed in the
water . . . "). The most complex use of water as symbol
occurs when Maria visits the Hoover Dam:

She began to feel the pressure of Hoover Dam, there on the
desert, began to feel the pressure and pull of the water. When
the pressure got great enough she drove out there. All that day
she felt the power surging through her own body. . . . Maria
walked through the chambers, stared at . . . the deep still
water. . . . She wanted to stay in the dam, lie on the great pipe
itself, but reticence saved her from asking.

The dam represents man's control over water, an essential
natural resource and a symbol of spiritual renewal. Its
compelling power enables Maria to forget momentarily
her own helplessness and desolation, and it functions sym-
bolically, as an image of order and control, to balance the
image of life as a random game of chance.

Water is the most positive symbol in the novel, and
Maria's attraction to it is an index to the depth and sensitivity of her character, to her potential for salvation. She
is not saved within the action of the novel, however, nor
will she be until she parts company with the Helenes and
Carters of the world, those true denizens of the spiritual
wasteland. Separating herself from them will not be
enough, however; she must also convert her nostalgic
yearning for the impossible (a quiet pastoral life with
Kate) into the initiative and energy to fashion the kind of
orderly life that is possible in the contemporary world.
Didion would be the first to acknowledge that this is no

mean task, and it is not a hopeful sign that no one in the novel leads such a life. But there is the water and the dam to show that order and control at least exist as metaphysical possibilities.

A modern work that invites comparison with *Play It As It Lays* is T. S. Eliot's *The Waste Land*, a poem that also renders the barrenness and lovelessness in contemporary life. Eliot shows, too, the lives without purpose, the sexual encounters without passion, the terror lying just beneath the surface of routine lives. Eliot believed that modern man could be saved only when willing to risk death by drowning, to heed the imperative of the thunder: to give, sympathize, and control. Maria Wyeth lacked control, but she demonstrated a capacity for sympathy totally lacking in her friends; in this capacity, as well as her willingness to face her own terror, Didion may see a slim but real hope.

Play It As It Lays was published to generally good reviews. John Leonard of *The New York Times* began his review with high praise:

There hasn't been another American writer of Joan Didion's quality since Nathanael West. She writes with a razor, carving her characters out of her perceptions with strokes so swift and economical that each scene ends almost before the reader is aware of it; and yet the characters go on bleeding afterwards.[5]

Other reviewers remark upon her precision of detail, the novel's swift pace, her sure presentation of the chilling deterioration of Maria's life. Guy Davenport of the *National Review* perhaps sums up the novel's achievement best: "Miss Didion is a writer who honors life, and who feels that its clarity and goodness have been blasted in our time."[6]

With the publication of *Play It As It Lays* in 1970 Didion became established as a major talent among American novelists. She had published two earlier books: *Run River*, her first novel, in 1963, and *Slouching Toward*

Bethlehem, a collection of essays, in 1968. The essays, in particular, earned her critical acclaim, but neither book reached the large audience that read *Play It As It Lays*. Many from that audience, having responded to the sheer power of the sharp prose with which Didion sculpts Maria Wyeth, turned to her earlier writings, especially *Run River*. As *Play It As It Lays* is dominated by the image of the arid deserts lying south of Los Angeles, *Run River* is united by the image of the rich Sacramento River and the fertile valley that it irrigates. Yet Lily McClellan, the heroine of *Run River*, is in some ways soulmate to Maria Wyeth, for she, too, incorporates within herself a set of specifically American illusions, myths learned in childhood, painfully tested in adulthood, and finally eroded by the currents of social and economic change.

3

Run River

Play It As It Lays takes place in a contemporary hell—the hell of Maria's mind, the hell of 130-degree temperatures on the desert, the hell of a bedroom where a doctor performs illegal abortions. Like the idea of hell, the action of the novel is linked to no highly specific time; it could have taken place in 1960 or in 1965 or in 1970. Although Didion refers to specific months, neither she nor any character in the novel makes a single reference to a specific year. The omission is surely deliberate; Didion wanted to portray a world whose inhabitants are unaware of social issues or political events at either the national or the local level. The total self-absorption of Maria and BZ and Helene is in fact one of the qualities which consigns them to hell.

Run River, on the other hand, is set in historical time. The novel is divided into three sections: both the first and last sections are entitled "August 1959," and the central section, chapters four through twenty-four, is entitled "1938–1959." Nor does the reader ever lose the sense of precise historical time; we know not only the month and year of major events in the novel, but the exact date (December 6, 1848) on which the first Knight died in California, even the year (1933) in which Walter Knight's mistress sold him 120 frontage feet of a downtown block in Sacramento. The inclusion of dates in *Run River* is just as deliberate as their exclusion from *Play It As It Lays*, for in *Run River* Didion dramatizes the impact of historical events, World War II and the housing and industrial expansion that followed in its wake, on two families that have lived in California's Sacramento Valley since the mid-nineteenth century.

To understand this story that takes place between 1938 and 1959 we must understand Didion's feelings about a major historical event that took place one hundred years earlier: the original settling of California. Didion has always been fascinated by the history of westward migration in America, the constant push through new frontiers that ended finally in California, the Eden that seemed to promise freedom and riches to those strong and determined enough to find it. She does not accept the romantic view of California's first settlers as heroic pioneers, however, nor does she believe that their deepest drive was for wealth or material gain.

Didion believes that Americans who kept pushing west sought something far less tangible than gold or fertile farmland, something they could not have articulated, but which might be identified as a new sense of self. The English novelist and critic D. H. Lawrence expressed a view of the European migration to the United States that is comparable to Didion's view of the American migration to California. Lawrence claimed that Europeans who came to America "came largely to get away—that most simple of motives. To get away. Away from what? In the long run, away from themselves. . . . To get away from everything they are and have been."[1] Pointing out New England's dark history of religious oppression, Lawrence dismissed the familiar notion that the "Pilgrim Fathers" came to the New World in search of freedom. They were only "escaped slaves," he contended, and their cries of freedom were merely "a rattling of chains."[2]

Didion believes that the early settlers of California, like the Pilgrim Fathers, misunderstood their own motives. While they talked about wanting gold or land,

they unconsciously sought a renewed identity that was no
more accessible in California than it had been in Kentucky or Tennessee or wherever they came from. Perhaps
it was even less accessible, Didion has suggested, for the
natural physical realities of the West, the mountains, the
desert, and the endless blue sky, are so overwhelming that
they diminish the individual, reducing him to insignificance. In a recent book review Didion testified to "that
vast emptiness at the center of the Western experience, a
nihilism antithetical not only to literature but to most
other forms of human endeavor, a dread so close to zero
that human voices fade out, trail off, like skywriting."[3]
The first settlers of California found fertile land, but they
could not find what they sought; in the end each of them
was alone with the same needs and fears that he brought
with him. Didion realizes the impossibility of defining
specifically what they were seeking, but her writings suggest that their restlessness may perhaps be laid to a
childish longing for an earthly paradise, an Eden where
their needs would be met without effort, their discontent
miraculously soothed.

They learned, of course, that the West could not be a
paradise for fallen man, and, having reached the Pacific,
they could search no further. Neither could they go back,
however, for they had paid an enormous price for coming. Didion has often recalled the experience of the
Donner–Reed party from Illinois, who set out for California in 1846: forced by blizzards to make camp in the
Sierras, forty of the original party of eighty-seven survived—by eating their own dead. Not every group paid
quite this high a price, of course, but every person who
made the trip faced risk and hardship difficult now even to
imagine. Perhaps the rich Sacramento Valley did appear
as a promised land after the trials of the wilderness;
perhaps the Edenic myth began with those who needed to
believe that the end of the journey justified what they had
endured along the way. Or perhaps the myth began not

with those hardy spirits who managed to reach California, but with their descendants several generations later, the inheritors of the vast ranches and orchards developed in the nineteenth century. In either case, Didion inherited the myth as a child in Sacramento, and not until she had lived almost ten years in New York did she clearly see the danger that lay in its ready acceptance. Lily Knight McClellan, the heroine of *Run River*, is a woman like many Didion knew; she is even, conceivably, the woman Didion might have become, had she not discovered literature at the age of twelve.

At the conclusion of *Run River*, waiting for the sheriff to come and discover the bodies of her husband and her lover, Lily realizes, perhaps too late, that the Sacramento Valley is not Eden, but rather a "void" onto which generations of Californians have projected their hopes and fantasies:

She, her mother, Everett, Martha, the whole family gallery: they carried the same blood, come down through twelve generations of circuit riders, county sheriffs, Indian fighters, country lawyers, Bible readers, one obscure United States Senator from a frontier state a long time ago; two hundred years of clearings in Virginia and Kentucky and Tennessee and then the break, the void into which they gave their rosewood chests, their silver brushes; the cutting clean which was to have redeemed them all. They had been a particular kind of people, their particular virtues called up by a particular situation, their particular flaws waiting there through all those years, unperceived, unsuspected. . . . What is it you want, she had asked Everett tonight. It was a question she might have asked them all.

Lily, Martha, and Everett do not ever define what they want, for they accept what they were taught: that their heritage of close families and rich farming land is all that one could want or need. The illusions that destroy Lily's marriage and leave Everett and his sister dead are corollaries of the myth that the valley is a second Eden. One of these illusions is that the valley is the center of the world and that nothing beyond it is either real or significant. Another is that the family is an inviolable unit whose members never hurt or betray each other. Lily Knight and Everett McClellan share these illusions as they share an almost identical family history.

Both families came to the valley in 1848, and pride in land and ancestry is strong in both. When Lily's father shows her the grave (on his property) of Matthew Broderick Knight, the first family member to die in California, Lily responds, "Sometimes I think this whole Valley belongs to me." Her father confirms her statement, adding, "We made it." Although they feel expansive about the valley, however, the Knights and the McClellans are terribly provincial about the rest of the world. Mr. McClellan believed that "Easterners fell into two camps: goddamn pansies and goddamn Jews," and Everett thinks of Eastern cities as "another world, a world teeming with immigrants and women who spent the day in art galleries and elevator operators who called you by name if you were a crack *Life* reporter."

Although Everett graduated from Stanford and Lily spent a year at Berkeley, they were often uncomfortable with their classmates, both Western urbanites who were adept at small talk and the bright offspring of Jewish liberals from the East. Everett has affairs with girls in each of these categories, but he realizes that they are not girls with whom he could live on the ranch. Knowing that he will spend his life as his father did, as a grower, he knows also that he will marry his childhood playmate Lily Knight: "Lily required no commitment: Lily was already there." Lily, only eighteen when he proposes to her, is not at all sure that she wants to marry Everett, but she sees no other future for herself and at last agrees to elope with him. Once married they both make the mistake of assuming that their lives are impervious to anything outside the valley. World War II affects them profoundly when Everett joins the army, and newcomers to the valley—entrepreneurs who come in the same spirit that their own

ancestors brought ninety years earlier—disturb their lives
even more deeply than the war.

Lily and Everett view the family much as they do the
valley, as a closed, perfect circle that cannot be penetrated
by outsiders. The father-daughter and the brother-sister
relationships are so close that they take on incestuous
overtones. Lily is so bound to her father that she cannot
bear to tell him she has promised to marry Everett, and
when she was a child Martha predicted that she would
marry her brother Everett as soon as Roosevelt was
removed from office (blaming Roosevelt for the ban
against sibling marriages, just as her father blamed him
for everything wrong with the country). When Lily and
Everett elope, Mr. Knight broods for days, and Martha
accuses Everett of deserting her.

The myth of the close-knit family is so strong in *Run
River* that betrayal cannot be dealt with, can scarcely even
be acknowledged. Lily's father has kept a mistress for
twelve years, but her mother not only denies this reality to
herself and to Lily but even defends Rita as a lady "from
an old, old family in the Valley . . . a family which
crossed the Great Plains a year before my own." Everett
never confronts Lily with his knowledge of her affairs
because to do so might rend the delicate fabric of their
relationship. Lily persists in sleeping with any man who
wants her, thinking that even though Everett knows of her
affairs, she can "make it all right, make everyone happy."

Both of these myths are shattered on an August evening in 1959 when Lily hears a shot "cracking reflexively
through all the years before, spinning through the
darkness between the games they had all played as
children and the games they played now, between the
child she had been and whoever she was now . . . " *Run
River*, like *Play It As It Lays*, begins with the end of the
action, the tragic culmination of the events of Lily's
and Everett's nineteen-year marriage, Everett's murder of
her lover.

Although the entire novel is written in the third person, Didion actually develops three distinct points of view in presenting the action. Of the total of twenty-six chapters, fifteen are narrated from Lily's point of view, six are written from Everett's point of view, and in five the author writes as omniscient narrator. So skillfully does Didion shift among these points of view that at times we are scarcely aware that she has done so. It is important to look at her narrative technique closely, however, for it is not only a means of developing character and theme. She also uses narrative technique to produce certain special effects: to suspend the action temporarily in order to let the reader see scenes from the past, to balance and juxtapose contrasting scenes, and to create here and there a satirical portrait.

In chapter one Didion focuses on the moment when Lily discovers that Everett's gun is not in the drawer where it belongs; she then freezes that moment while Lily recalls each incident of the day. Two contrasting events stand out for her: her lovemaking with Everett in the afternoon, and the call from Channing that she took during dinner, when she agreed to meet him later on the dock. Lily does not want to meet Channing, but she cannot say "no"; her love and guilt, however, are all directed toward Everett, who she knows is not deceived.

In chapters two and three the reader is with Everett, sitting on the dock, flooded with memories very different from Lily's, thinking not of Channing's body drifting under the dock but of the hops drying in the kiln, of his sister Sarah not understanding why he refused to sell the ranch, and of the pain he had felt earlier that night when he realized that Lily had left the Templeton's party alone to keep her appointment with Channing. By presenting the contrasting viewpoints of Lily and Everett, Didion dramatizes the tremendous emotional distance between them, distance created by their inability to find words with which to communicate either their love or their pain to the other.

Leaving Everett and Lily on the dock, Didion then turns time backward to 1938, the year of Lily's sixteenth birthday. Didion becomes an omniscient narrator here (chapter four), for she wants the reader to see more than Lily could possibly have understood at that age. She shows us first that the reign of Walter Knight (his name is, of course, symbolic) and men like him is reaching an end, for far from being destined to become governor of California, as Lily had assumed he would, Knight loses his bid for reelection to the state legislature that year to an opponent who stands for "the little fellow" and refers to Walter as the representative of "the robber land barons." Didion also shows us that the marriage of Walter and Edith Knight is sustained largely by outward forms, by public displays of affection, for Walter has for twelve years been "keeping company" with Rita Blanchard, a close family friend and cousin of the McClellans. Didion's portrait of Edith Knight is almost purely satirical; she is the proper Sacramento matron incarnate, fully aware of her husband's relationship with Rita, but equally aware that the subject cannot delicately be discussed. On the one occasion when she makes reference to the time that Walter spends on Thirty-eighth Street (Rita's home), she is immediately "flushed and rigid with regret as if with fever. Without looking at her, Walter Knight reached across the table and touched her hand. 'Sarcasm,' he said, 'has never been your *forté*.' Edith Knight stiffened her shoulders and picked up her water goblet. 'The word is *forte*, Walter,' she said, entirely herself again. 'Quite unaccented.'"

Failing to see the tension beneath the placid surface of her family life, Lily grew up adoring her father, trusting him absolutely. When he reminds her that she has descended from people "who've wanted things and got them," Lily confesses that she doesn't know what she wants. "I'll do the worrying," he responds. "You know that." So Lily is raised to believe that she needn't struggle, needn't make choices, for someone will be there to take care of her. In Eden, of course, choice is unnecessary, since one is surrounded only by that which is good; and struggle is equally inappropriate, since God (or Walter Knight) will provide for all one's needs.

Didion assumes the omniscient viewpoint in chapter four to show the reader that, contrary to Lily's perception of them, Walter Knight is a weak man and Edith Knight, a frivolous woman. The next three chapters are told from Lily's limited point of view. As a freshman at Berkeley she does not know how to respond to either academic or social demands, for the only demand she has learned to meet is her mother's insistence on ladylike behavior. No one in her family takes her education seriously in any case, and she decides not to return after the first year. She has been home only a week when her childhood friend Everett McClellan calls to ask her to ride to town with him. After returning to his father's ranch they swim across the Sacramento River and lie on the far bank, where Lily, who has been planning all year to lose her virginity, whispers, "I wish you would kiss me" to the young man who, having spoken fewer than twenty words to her all day, appears not to be excessively demanding.

But Everett is ready to settle down and become a rancher; by July he is putting pressure on Lily to marry him. Lily isn't at all sure that she wants to, but, having slept with him twenty-seven times, she feels that she must; marriage to Everett seems to her "as inescapable as the ripening of the pears, as fated as the exile from Eden." Because she cannot bring herself to tell her parents of their plans, toward the end of the summer Everett drives her to Reno, where they are married by a justice of the peace. It is striking that neither during their courtship nor on their honeymoon do they exchange confidences about their feelings, or even have a conversation of more than fifteen words. They are really still children, for they have not taken the crucial adolescent step of "breaking away"

from their parents' values in order to form their own. Or
at least Lily is still a child; the reader does not yet know
Everett as a young man of twenty-two, since the entire
account of their courtship is presented from Lily's point
of view.

Life at the McClellan ranch is truly an "exile from
Eden" for Lily, for Everett is withdrawn in the presence of
his father, and, since their housekeeper takes care of the
house, Lily has no role to play. Her communication with
Everett remains essentially nonverbal, although often
tender; when she becomes pregnant and is frightened of
childbirth, he brings flowers to her each morning in bed.
When their son Knight is born they lie in bed in the
mornings with him between them, but the bedroom is
their only haven from the aggressive bossiness of both
Everett's father and his sister Martha, who seems to
regard the child as her own.

When she becomes pregnant a second time, Lily
looks at her life from the outside and concludes that she is
now a "river matron" (the year is 1942; Lily is twenty
years old). Uncertain about the precise role she should be
playing, she recalls the huge parties given by her mother
and decides to expand her social life. Accordingly, she
orders "six hundred sheets of pale blue letter paper
monogrammed L. K. McC., four hundred lined enve-
lopes engraved *McClellan's Landing, California* . . . and a
small book similar to one used by Mrs. Roosevelt's social
secretary to record the . . . favorite menus of all one's
guests."

Just as Lily decides to behave in a manner appropriate to the wife of a landed gentleman, Didion manipulates the plot of the novel to show that the preeminence of
landed aristocracy in Sacramento has ended. Walter
Knight and Rita Blanchard are killed in an accident that
plunges their car into the Sacramento River. In the
chapter describing the discovery of the accident and the
reactions of Edith and Lily, Didion becomes omniscient

narrator once again. This shift in viewpoint permits her some fine satire of the tourists who discover the accident (the woman interprets the lights flickering through the water as an ad for a Giant Orange drink), as well as an objective view of Lily's terror (making marmalade for her father when she hears the news, she bites her knuckles to keep from screaming) and Edith's decorum ("The Lord gives it and takes it, Mr. Paley," she responds to the coroner's assistant at the morgue where she has come to identify the bodies). The funeral itself is a ritual marking the end of an era:

> From all over the Valley and from the Sierra foothills the family came; everyone from the river came and everyone from town came. . . . the Governor came, and the bartender from the Senator Hotel came.

Few of the mourners who recount to Edith their memories of Walter's generous deeds ("the litany of Walter Knight's shining hours . . . ") realize that the war which has already sent ripples through the valley will in a few years produce waves powerful enough to erode the social and economic bases of the valley's huge ranches and orchards, the bases of lives like Walter Knight's.

When Didion returns the point of view to Lily, it is three months after her father's death, and she has just given birth to a daughter. Lying in the hospital bed waiting for Everett, she addresses again the problem that she tried previously to resolve by becoming a "river matron," the problem of her essential identity. She envies the nuns in the Catholic hospital the certainty with which they play their nursing roles. "I should have taken the Holy Ghost not Everett," she thinks, for she and her husband rarely communicate now, and when they make love she has the fantasy that she is someone else. She knows that something went wrong, but not how or when it went wrong: "She wanted now only to see her father, to go back to that country in time where no one makes mistakes."

Lily is beginning to understand that paradise exists not as a place, but only as a time—the time of infancy, when a child's needs are met despite his inability to articulate them, his total helplessness.

Lily mourns her father even more deeply when Everett enlists in the army two months after Julie's birth. The war in Europe seems remote from the Sacramento Valley, and she views Everett's act as outright desertion. Closeted in the McClellan house with Everett's querulous father and two babies, she spends her afternoons with her mother and her evenings playing hearts with her father-in-law. She drifts into an affair with a neighbor, but does not feel deeply involved and continues to write Everett every night. When her sister-in-law graduates from Davis and rejoins the household, family tensions mount, for Mr. McClellan feels only contempt for Martha's boy-friend Ryder Channing, a soldier from Tennessee stationed in the valley.

During this time Lily's inability to be emotionally close to women works against both her and Martha. When Martha learns of Lily's affair with Joe Templeton, she is at first enraged and tells Lily that she has no right to Everett; she later apologizes, aware of her brother's love for Lily. Lily, frightened of Martha's anger, neither explains nor defends herself; when Martha relents and confesses to Lily her own fears that she will not be able to create for herself "a nice ordered life right here on the river," Lily turns away from her confidences, unable to deal with the emotions of another woman. Had Lily and Martha been able to communicate with and support each other, Lily's loneliness might have been transcended, and Martha's later suicide averted.

During the summer and fall of 1944 the children have one illness after another, and Martha's emotional state becomes more and more chaotic. It is at this point, while Lily is begging Everett to use his holiday pass to come home for a few days, that Didion shifts from Lily's to Everett's point of view. Ironically, it is Everett who now occupies a kind of paradise (as a noncombatant soldier, his only responsibility is to obey orders), while life at the McClellan ranch has become a form of hell. Contented with the orderliness of his life at Fort Bliss (an obvious pun), feeling Lily's appeals as threats to that order, he responds to her with the cliché, "Don't you know there's a war going on?" Secure in the knowledge that his absence is "blessed by all the Allied Powers," he enjoys lying in his bunk at night spinning elaborate fantasies of ways to develop the ranch. He is forced to apply for a hardship discharge, however, when his father dies suddenly of a stroke.

Arriving home, Everett is startled to realize that Lily was telling the truth about the deteriorated condition of the ranch; he immediately sets about the task of restoring order. He does not address the equally compelling problems in his relationship with Lily, though, nor does he talk to Martha about her troubled relationship with Ryder Channing. He often hears Lily crying at night, but is afraid to ask way, afraid to confront her anger and loneliness. He knows of her affair with Joe Templeton but tries to dismiss it as a vagary of war. He does not realize that the affair has continued (nor does the reader), until several months after his return, when Lily tells him that she's pregnant and (she thinks) not by him.

In the next two chapters Didion develops a sharp sympathy for Everett, totally overwhelmed by feelings of inadequacy. He spends the night that he learns of Lily's pregnancy drinking bourbon and looking at pictures of all of them as children, wondering, as Lily did in the hospital in an earlier scene, what has gone wrong.

He wished that he could go upstairs to Lily, tell her that it would be all right. . . . But somewhere they had stopped listening to each other, and so he remained downstairs in a paralysis not of anger but of lassitude and pride.

He, too, has an Edenic vision of their childhood, a nostalgic desire to bring back the past. While Lily mourned the loss of her father, Everett misses the birthday parties that the snapshots have recalled to him, the games of hide-and-seek that ended with all players "home free."

Everett did not feel angry with Lily about the pregnancy, yet anger was the feeling he expressed. He felt safer, less vulnerable, in showing anger than in showing his real feelings of inadequacy and hurt pride. Yet anger was the signal Lily picked up and responded to; when Everett returns from the fields the next day, he discovers that she has gone to San Francisco for an abortion, leaving him a note in their bed: "Everett darling I'll try to make everything all right. Please. L." Illegal abortion is the last solution he would have chosen for the problem, for not only does it place Lily's welfare at risk, but he wanted more children, and it might, after all, have been his. He does not share these feelings with her either; when she gets home, he puts her to bed and sleeps himself in his father's bedroom. He and Lily drift further and further apart on waves of misunderstanding, confused and unspoken emotion.

Didion's alternation of Lily's and Everett's points of view serves well to reveal them to the reader and also to dramatize their growing estrangement. In chapters eighteen through twenty, which take place four years after Lily's abortion, Didion becomes omniscient narrator again, this time to portray the emotional disintegration of Everett's sister Martha, a process Martha hides not only from Lily and Everett, but even from herself. For four years Martha has been conducting an affair with Captain Ryder Channing. Devious but charming, vaguely involved in real estate, Ryder expends much energy cultivating rich and propertied women. Unlike anyone she grew up with, Ryder puzzles, captivates, and enrages Martha. She disapproves of him thoroughly, but cannot extricate herself from the affair. When she discovers that he is engaged to marry a wealthy heiress, she covers over her grief and rage with frenzied activity—parties, shop-

ping trips, and the Junior League. Striving for a "pervasive contempt" of men, she feels after several months
that she is no longer vulnerable to either sexual love or
sexual hate. This defense is shattered, though, on the
night that Channing, now married, stops by the ranch
and seduces her without love or tenderness. That night
Martha takes out a boat alone on the river at high flood
and drowns.

Martha is a victim of many forces: her own unac-
knowledged incestuous love for her brother; her restless
ambition, for which she finds no acceptable outlet; and
the social changes of war that brought Ryder Channing, a
man untutored in the chivalrous attitudes toward women
prevailing in the valley, into her life. To Everett, raised in
the tradition of chivalry that Channing lacked, Martha's
death meant his own failure to protect her, and his guilt
becomes one more burden not shared with Lily, one more
unresolved feeling driving them apart.

Martha dies in 1949; during the next ten years,
presented from Lily's point of view, Everett becomes
more compulsive about managing the ranch and more
withdrawn from Lily and the children. Divorced from the
heiress, Channing reappears in 1953 and convinces Lily
that he needs her; they commence an affair that continues
until he is killed by Everett six years later. In a pattern
similar to that of Maria and Carter in *Play It As It Lays*,
Lily and Everett have bitter quarrels in which they ac-
cuse each other of not caring; unlike Maria and Carter,
however, they usually make up in a mood of tender
remorse.

At last Didion arrives at the summer of 1959, the
season with which the novel opened. Lily's and Everett's
daughter Julie, now sixteen, has her mother's fragile
beauty and tentative gestures. Their son Knight is eighteen and will be going east to Princeton in the fall. It has
been a summer of tension and conflict, especially between
Everett and his son. When Everett refuses to help Knight

get his driver's license reinstated after a minor accident, Knight taunts his father with his passive indifference to Lily's affairs. After several days Knight apologizes to his parents for his behavior, but the tension is not dissipated, for the most burning issue between father and son—Everett's certain knowledge that Knight has no wish to be a rancher, that he will someday sell the property—is never discussed.

With Everett's shooting of Channing, the novel comes full circle. In the penultimate chapter Everett says goodbye to Lily, lovingly, and in the final chapter Lily hears the shot with which he ends his own life. Finding his lifeless body on the dock, she speaks to it of early, happier times together, hoping that "she could somehow imprint her ordinary love upon his memory through all eternity, hoped he would rise thinking of her, we were each other . . . "

Lily Knight McClellan is one of Didion's most successful fictional characters, a convincing product of her time and place, literally a Lily-of-the-Valley. Raised in the thirties and forties when middle-class young women throughout the country were taught to seek fulfillment through husband and children, she drifts into marriage and motherhood while still a child herself, too inexperienced to understand that Everett's personality is fundamentally cold and withdrawn. When Everett seems not to need her, she turns to men who do—Joe Templeton, whose wife preferred drink to sex, and Ryder Channing, who soothed his business failures with passionate affairs. While men in Lily's culture were expected to be growers, ranchers or politicians, women were expected to serve men's sexual and emotional needs.

Run River was written before the current women's movement; it was in fact published in the same year (1963) as *The Feminine Mystique*, the book that signaled the start of the movement. In the portrait of Lily Didion dramatized the very mystique of which Friedan wrote, the myth that a woman finds her real self in husband, home, and children. Passive and insecure, her father's "princess" and her husband's "baby," Lily lives the mystique to the end of her marriage, splashing Joy on her neck and putting on her high heels even after she hears the shot that she suspects is Everett's revenge on her lover.

The "feminine mystique" encouraged women to look to men for validation of their essential worth. Both Lily and Martha used men as mirrors in which they sought the reflected self; if their men found them charming and appealing, then they knew that they were. Pretty and naturally shy, Lily had in some ways an easier time than her sister-in-law. Bright and aggressive, an enormously successful student in college, Martha threatened men, causing them to withdraw from her. Convinced that neither her father nor Everett nor Ryder loved her, she punished them by taking her own life.

Lacking close female friends, lacking real intimacy with her mother, Lily imagines that other women are better satisfied in their roles than she is in hers:

Mary Knight, her mother, the nuns in the corridor: they all seemed to know something she did not. Well, she had at least given Everett what he wanted. Even Martha could scarcely have given him two children. But she could not escape the uneasy certainty that she had done so herself only by way of some intricate deception, that her entire life with Everett was an improvisation dependent upon cues she might one day fail to hear, characterizations she might at any time forget.

The reason that Lily depends upon cues from others is, of course, that she is not expressing—has in fact never found—the real person beneath the "princess" and and "baby." There are hints that the real Lily is intelligent and responsive—she certainly acts fast when her baby's life is threatened by a deep cut—but she seldom receives cues as clear as a bleeding child. She allowed her father to define her as a child; this fact explains her reaction to his death:

"I'm not myself if my father's dead." She then allowed Everett to define her as his lover. But when he withdraws from her after their marriage she loses her sense of self and must attempt to regain it through the attentions of other men. Ironically, Everett's suicide is an expression of love for her and the children, an attempt to protect them from the potentially hideous ordeal of a murder trial in the course of which Lily's affairs would become public knowledge. It is perhaps for this reason that Lily stands strong and calm at the end of the novel; Everett has at last rendered his love for her permanent and inviolable.

In style *Run River* is the most expansive of Didion's novels; the narrator knows and tells all, in a voice that is calm, smooth, and leisurely. The reader knows Lily perhaps better than any other Didion character, for much of the novel's action is filtered through her consciousness, and nothing about her past or present is held back. Whereas we see Maria Wyeth at close range for only a year, we observe Lily, at intervals, over twenty-one years. In one of the more perceptive reviews that the novel received, Guy Davenport praised Didion for "an uncommon grasp of place and character."[4] In *Run River* Didion called upon her earliest memories of the Sacramento Valley; although twelve years younger than Lily, she had relatives whose provincial views matched those of the McClellans, and she was not too young to observe the sweeping changes that took place in the valley after the war.

At one level *Run River* is an American period piece, dramatizing the events and illusions of a particular time and place in American history. The myth of the feminine mystique, which flourished in the United States between 1930 and 1965, can be explained by various historical circumstances: reaction against the first women's movement and fantasies of home and hearth woven by men who fought in the two world wars are among those circumstances. The other illusions by which the two families in

the novel try to live their lives—the notions that both the
family and the valley are safely insulated from outside
forces—were also the products of a particular time and, in
this case, a more local place. In several essays, Didion has
described the history of Sacramento, the settlers who
came in the mid-nineteenth century,

the farmers, the people who for two hundred years had been
moving west on the frontier, the peculiar flawed strain who had
cleared Virginia, Kentucky, Missouri; they made Sacramento a
farm town. Because the land was rich, Sacramento became
eventually a rich farm town, which meant houses in town,
Cadillac dealers, a country club. In that gentle sleep Sacramento
dreamed until perhaps 1950, when . . . Sacramento woke to the
fact that the outside world was moving in, fast and hard. At the
moment of its waking Sacramento lost, for better or worse, its
character.[5]

Although Ryder Channing dies, he is the emblem of
change that destroys the McClellan family; with Everett's
death the old Sacramento of rich growers and ranchers
also dies, to be replaced by the Sacramento of rapid housing development and engineers from Aerojet General and
Douglas Aircraft. All over the United States, of course,
farmland gave way to sprawling cities and the industries
that supported them, but in Sacramento the change was
characterized by a particular violence, because it chal-
lenged the illusions of people like Martha and Everett that
the valley was the fixed and immutable center around
which the earth turned.

As she does in *Play It As It Lays*, Didion in *Run River*
weaves specifically American themes with universal
spiritual and moral ones. The most universal of the
novel's themes, the relentless power of time, is suggested
by Lily's diamond wristwatch, by the office clock that
Martha finds intolerable, and by Didion's precise ac-
counting for time (the novel opens with the sentence,
"Lily heard the shot at seventeen minutes to one.") The
principal metaphor for time, however, is the Sacramento

River itself. As it irrigates the crops, thus bringing the pears and the hops to fruition, the river represents the positive power of time; as it reaches flood levels and drowns the careless swimmer, it represents time's destructive power.

Didion sets the Sacramento River over and against the unreal Eden of which Lily, Martha, and Everett dream. The river is an appropriate symbol to combat the Edenic myth, for time and change as we know them did not exist in the original earthly paradise. Although the sun rose and set in Eden, aging and death were unknown before man's sin; together with other forms of suffering, they are realities of a fallen world.

The characters in *Run River* who drown in the depths of the Sacramento or die on its banks are those whom time has defeated: Walter Knight, the "easy loser"; Martha McClellan, who desperately wanted "an orderly life on the river"; Ryder Channing, who has failed as both husband and real estate speculator; and Everett McClellan, who thought his problems would disappear if he simply ignored them. Ultimately, of course, time vanquishes everyone; all life, all relationships, must fall victim to the passage of the years. But time is especially unkind to people who live in the past rather than the present and future. When Everett takes his sister Sarah to the airport after his father's funeral, he weeps as her plane leaves the runway, "not so much for his father as for Sarah's defection, because she had lost all memory of the family they had been." But of all the McClellan siblings only Sarah, who turned toward the present and the future rather than the past, survived.

Martha and Everett cannot accept the loss that time and aging inevitably bring, the loss of childhood visions, the permanent separation from the dead whom one has loved. Both Lily and her mother have a resilience, an ability to live in the present, that the McClellans lacked. Deprived of her husband, Mrs. Knight takes consolation in the Dodgers, newly arrived in Los Angeles from Brooklyn; for all her passivity, Lily has more insight into the nature of time than any other character in the novel:

Everything changes, everything changed: summer evenings driving downriver to auctions, past the green hops in leaf, blackbirds flying up from the brush in the dry twilight air, red Christmas tree balls glittering in the firelight . . . all gone. . . . Your father no longer lulls you with his father's bourbon, brought out for comfort at Christmas and funerals. Nobody chooses it but nothing can halt it. . . . You now share not only that blood but that loss.

There is in *Run River* a suggestion that mortal loss may be redeemed in an afterlife, that time itself may one day be vanquished by eternity. At her father's funeral Lily memorizes a passage from the Order for the Burial of the Dead in the Book of Common Prayer—"For a thousand years in thy sight are but as yesterday when it is past, and as a watch in the night." When Martha drowns, Everett insists on burying her on the ranch; only Lily and their foreman are present to hear the child's prayer that he speaks over her: "Gentle Jesus, meek and mild. . . . Look upon a little child. Pity her simplicity and suffer her to come to thee." Thinking of the isolation of Christ on the cross, Lily prays for Everett when he asks to be left alone after the shooting: "Drive far away our ghostly foe and thine abiding peace bestow."

There is also in the novel a recurrent image that may hint of an ultimate triumph, whether man's or God's, over time. The image is one of light shining through the river water. When Walter Knight's car jumps the road into the river, the car's headlights are the means of its discovery. Didion describes the scene as it appeared to the tourist who stopped to investigate: "The light filtered up through layer upon layer of current and cross-current, and flickered all about the channel . . . " A similar image occurs after Everett shoots Channing, when he notices "Channing's flashlight, still burning, its thin light filtering

through three inches of muddy water . . . " At the very
least these images suggest that the passage of time is not
without hope, that man's spirit may in some form survive
his life on earth. Although Didion has never avowed belief
in a deity, she admits to fondness for the words of the
Episcopal service; it is perhaps significant that her favorite
passage refers explicitly to an eternal principle that
transcends time and change: "As it was in the beginning,
is now, and ever shall be, world without end."[6]

The spiritual and the psychological dimensions of
Didion's characters cannot finally be separated. Lily and
Everett each cling to a distorted, Edenic view of their
childhood, a view perhaps determined a century before
their marriage, when their ancestors crossed the plains
and the mountains in search of the earthly paradise. The
passions and errors of their adult life signaled their expul-
sion from the perfect garden, but by the end of the novel
they have a measure of the self-knowledge that in Chris-
tian theology serves as compensation to man for his fall
from grace. Everett recognizes that his real enemy is not
Channing, but the "nameless fury which pursued him ten,
twenty, a good many years before." Lily sees that her
weakness has had tragic consequences and that she can
help Everett now only by praying and letting him go.
They are redeemed, too, by their actions at the close of
the novel: Everett's reassuring Lily that he has always
known of her love for him, and Lily holding his body
against the dark and rising to face the uncertain future.

Run River received scant notice in the press upon its
publication in the spring of 1963. The *Library Journal* saw
promise in its "impeccable local color,"[7] but the *New Yorker*
in a brief review dismissed its characters as "people who
get through life instead of living it."[8] Although published
only four years after the date of the fictional events of the
novel, it seemed not to be a novel for its time. In the
spring of 1963, already torn by a bitterly fought civil
rights campaign in the South, Americans were growing

uneasy about events in Vietnam; the politically quiet fifties had receded into the past, and World War II seemed
a century away. Had it not been Didion's first novel,
serious critics might have seen that it was not simply a
novel about a California province. To speak of its "local
color" is to misunderstand the novel completely: Lily
Knight's conflicts about her role were those of two decades
of American women, and Everett McClellan's ferocious
possessiveness toward his land is an instance of the American myth that proclaims that man feels a satisfying com-
munion with soil that he owns and tills himself. Lily and
Everett did have some notions that were peculiar to Californians, but their deepest illusions—that a woman must
have a man to protect her, that the family is an inviolable
unit, that a man can find salvation in work, especially
work on his own land—were American to the core.

Didion's profound insight into the American
character is fundamentally an understanding of the illusions that our collective and individual histories have
fostered. In *A Book of Common Prayer* she explores yet
another set of illusions, those of social, scientific, and
technological progress, the belief that the future will be a
continuation of the upward spiral that constitutes history.
As *Run River* is her realistic response to the feminine
mystique and the Edenic romance of land, and *Play It As
It Lays* confronts the myths of power and success, so her
third work of fiction attacks the myth that is perhaps the
most deep-rooted of all, the myth of the power of scientific
knowledge to explain human life and personality.

4

A Book of Common Prayer

In *The White Album*, her collection of essays published in 1979, Didion stated that the decade of the sixties in the United States was so afflicted by disorder and violence that no one she knew was surprised by the brutal "Manson murders" at the home of Sharon Tate in August 1969. The sixties was the decade of political assassinations (John F. Kennedy, Martin L. King, Robert F. Kennedy), of war in Vietnam, of student riots culminating in the deaths of four students shot by National Guardsmen at Kent State University in May 1970. It was also the decade of flower children, young people who dropped out of school or work and simply drifted, often on a wave of drugs. Large numbers of America's youth were engaged in a bitter cold war against the Establishment, and in response the Establishment itself was torn into factions.

A Book of Common Prayer is Didion's fictional tribute to the chaos of the sixties. Institutions like the family, faltering in *Run River*, are so shapeless in this novel as to be scarcely recognizable, and the novel has no reassuring symbol of permanence like a river, no sheriff to represent order, no Edenic vision, however nostalgic. In *A Book of Common Prayer* the life of every character is touched by political violence. The main character, Charlotte Douglas, is the mother of a student rebel turned outlaw; the narrator and Charlotte's counterpart in Central America, Grace Strasser-Mendana, is also the mother of a revolutionary, although he is less idealistic than his American counterpart. Leonard Douglas, Charlotte's husband, is a well-known lawyer who espouses liberal causes and, without apparent sense of conflict, arranges for the purchase of guns for international revolutionary and counterrevolutionary groups. Against the chaos of these lives Didion projects a moral vision informed by existential concepts of the human community. The novel's themes are thus timeless and universal as well as contemporary and American.

A Book of Common Prayer is Didion's most ambitious and complex novel to date. It has a large cast of characters, four of whom are fully developed (Charlotte, Grace, Leonard, and Warren Bogart, Charlotte's first husband) and a multiple setting, with scenes in San Francisco, New York City, and several southern United States cities interlaced with scenes in Central American countries, especially Boca Grande, the fictitious Central American country serving as a focus of the novel's action. The novel's narration is also complex, for it combines two narrative threads: the first is an account of the life of Charlotte Douglas from the moment when the FBI arrive at her house in San Francisco to the time of her death; the second is an account of the changes that take place in Grace's attitudes as she tells Charlotte's story.

These two narrative threads provide one structural principle of the novel. Its major structural principle, however, is thematic; each of the novel's six parts is dominated by one or two themes that the narrator stresses, linking them to herself and the other characters, particularly Charlotte Douglas. The novel's thematic organization, in fact, takes precedence over all else, including the chronological order of events. Thus Charlotte's story is presented in bits and pieces rather than in an orderly progression through beginning, middle, and end. After demonstrating how the novel is organized around its themes, I will analyze the two narrative threads to show how theme and narrative technique work together to reveal character and create a coherent pattern of ideas.

The narrator of *A Book of Common Prayer* is Grace Strasser-Mendana, a well-published anthropologist from Colorado who gave up her profession in her thirties and married a wealthy planter from Boca Grande. Now widowed and dying of cancer, she has decided to spend her remaining days in Boca Grande because she finds peace in the country's "opaque equatorial light." Grace tells us that the novel is her "witness" to Charlotte Douglas, who came to Boca Grande as a tourist and remained there for almost a year before she was killed in a revolution.

In part one of the novel Charlotte arrives in Boca Grande and establishes herself as a permanent sojourner, has an affair with Grace's brother-in-law, Victor, and compels the narrator's interest by her odd mixture of strength and weakness and her fixation upon an illusory past in which she and her daughter Marin were inseparable.

The central theme in part one is history, especially history as biography. Grace opens the novel with a brief summary of Charlotte's personal history and then summarizes her own. She states several times that Boca Grande has no history; what she means is that it has no early patriots, no national heroes, no known founding fathers. She gives an account of its recent past, which consists of elaborate roadway and building projects aborted after the assassination of President Luis, also her brother-in-law, in 1959. Grace wants the reader to understand that the setting for the story of Charlotte Douglas is not a romantic one.

In various chapters of part one Grace presents different kinds of historical data concerning Charlotte Douglas. Chapter 3 is an account of information revealed on her passport (nationality, occupation, places traveled);

chapter 11 is a list of possessions found on her person when she died. This objective data is contrasted with Grace's observations of Charlotte's behavior, both at a cocktail party and during a more private visit. The emphasis on history in part one shows Grace's view of her role: as detached, objective historian, she will tell the story of Charlotte Douglas. She claims that " 'the narrator' plays no motive role in this narrative, nor would I want to." Grace returns to the theme of history in part six when trying to determine whether Charlotte's own version of her past can be trusted.

The dominant theme of part two of *A Book of Common Prayer* is what Grace calls "sexual current"—sex as a powerful motive in human behavior. Both Charlotte's seductive behavior and her attitudes toward her sexual partners are detailed in this section. Although she sleeps with both Victor (Grace's brother-in-law) and Gerardo (Grace's son), Charlotte's attitude toward these affairs is not casual:

> . . . I have never known anyone who regarded the sexual connection as quite so unamusing a contract. So dark and febrile and outside the range of the normal did all aspects of this contract seem to Charlotte that she was for example incapable of walking normally across a room in the presence of two men with whom she had slept. . . . Her body went stiff, as if convulsed by the question of who had access to it and who did not.

Much of the action of part two takes place in San Francisco almost a year before Charlotte's arrival in Boca Grande. In her house on California Street Charlotte learns of the disappearance of her eighteen-year-old daughter Marin after the bombing of the Transamerica Building, is pursued by Warran Bogart, Marin's father and her first husband, and, five weeks after hearing Marin's taped voice speaking revolutionary rhetoric, she leaves Leonard Douglas, pregnant with his child. Although Charlotte dislikes Warren, she cannot resist his persistent efforts at seduction, perhaps because he wants her sexually so much more than Leonard does, or perhaps because he was her first lover. When Grace tells Charlotte about a primitive village in which girls are "ritually cut on the inner thigh by their first sexual partners," Charlotte responds, "That's pretty much what happens everywhere, isn't it? . . . Somebody cuts you? Where it doesn't show?"

Thus sex is linked to wounds and, by implication, to death, since Warren's frenzied sexual activity is his response to the knowledge that his death is imminent. In Warren's case the certainty of death leads to sexual intensity; in Charlotte's case sexual behavior leads to death, since her affairs with Victor and Gerardo are the probable reason for her murder. The themes are also linked in the dreams of "infant death and sexual surrender" that Grace and Charlotte both experience.

The theme of death is continued in part three with the death of Charlotte's prematurely born baby girl in Mérida. The dominant theme of part three, however, is aimless drifting, as Grace traces backward Charlotte's travels from the time she left the clinic where her baby was born to her arrival in Boca Grande. Leaving New Orleans with the doomed baby, Charlotte drifts south, first to Mérida, where she holds the baby in her arms when it is seized with convulsions and dies, then to Antigua, where she sits by the sea with the "sense that she could swim from where she was to somewhere else, but she had no idea what lay out there, or in what direction she was staring," and finally to Guadaloupe, where an Air France crash leads her to wonder if Marin might have been on the plane. This brief section of the novel is pervaded by a sense of vast perilous space through which Charlotte drifts, spinning fantasies of Marin's drifting: "Marin was loose in the world and could leave it any time and Charlotte would have no way of knowing."

The fourth section of *A Book of Common Prayer* is dominated by the related themes of chaos and physical decay. Chapter 1 opens with ugly images of physical corruption in Boca Grande:

> Fevers relapse here.
> Bacteria proliferate.
> Termites' eat the presidential palace, rust eats my Oldsmobile. . . .
> The bite of one fly deposits an egg which in its pupal stage causes human flesh to suppurate.
> The bite of another deposits a larval worm which three years later surfaces on and roams the human eyeball.

This corruption in the physical world is matched by the decay of social norms and personal relationships. Most of the action in this section takes place in the southern United States, where Charlotte wanders for five months with Warren, alternately tied to him by a sexual bond and hating him for his crude and outrageous behavior. Warren violates social codes not only by inviting himself and Charlotte to the homes of his friends for extended visits, but also by seducing "their host's wife or sister or recently divorced niece." One of the most extended scenes of social disorder in this section is a dinner that Grace attends in New Orleans several months after Charlotte has left Warren. Grace is there to renegotiate a copra contract with Morgan Fayard; Warren is there, an uninvited guest, apparently to embarrass the Fayards and discomfort as many people as possible. Before dinner he taunts Adele Fayard with allusions to a man she has been seeing, knowing that he can provoke Morgan into railing about "West Texas trash"; during dinner he forces the young woman with him to recite poetry and play a single tune on the piano. Turning to Grace, he aptly describes the situation he has created, "Doesn't this put you in mind of some third-rate traveling circus?" His body afflicted by cancer, corrupted morally as well as physically, Warren Bogart is the very embodiment of decadence.

In part five the social chaos deepens to become actual

violence, and the physical disintegration stressed in part
four is matched by a gradual disintegration of Charlotte's
personality. Since Didion leads the reader to compare
social disorder in the United States with that occurring in
Boca Grande, it is useful to recall her own statement
about a trip she made to Columbia in 1973:

In North America, social tensions that arise tend to be undercut
and co-opted quite soon, but in Latin America there does not
seem to be any political machinery for delaying the revolution.
Everything is thrown into bold relief. There is a collapsing of
time. Everything is both older than you could ever know, and it
started this morning.[1]

In comparison with the United States, social and political
tensions in Boca Grande are "thrown into bold relief" by
their greater violence and sharper finality. Warren Bogart
humiliates his friends and, on occasion, strikes his
girlfriend, but in Boca Grande Victor tries to murder his
brother. Although the student protest movement of the
sixties deeply affects the politics of the United States, in
Boca Grande the revolution fomented by Gerardo and
Antonio causes the violent overthrow of the government.
Thus it is appropriate that most of section five, the most
violent and ominous portion of the novel, should take
place in Boca Grande.

   In chapter 1 of this section Grace identifies the signs
of coming violence: "There is an occasional tank on the
Avenida Centrale. Sentries with carbines appear on the
roof of the Presidential palace." Charlotte displays more
public energy than ever, but her emotional stability,
always precarious, is now breaking down. Unable to sleep
at night, she goes out to the movies or calls the California
Highway Patrol in San Francisco and listens to the taped
"road condition" report. A bomb explodes in the clinic
where she works, killing four persons; she drags three
people to safety, but remembers afterwards only that she
was changing a tampax at the time of the explosion and

consequently bled all over the floor. Leonard Douglas comes to Boca Grande to tell Charlotte that Warren is dead, that he knows where Marin is, and that she must leave the country. But Charlotte prefers to pretend that nothing is happening; she regrets that she cannot "arrange an evening" for Leonard, and on the night that Grace leaves the country she pins a gardenia on her dress as a farewell gesture.

Charlotte's menstrual blood in part five prefigures her death in the final section, which represents the culmination of all earlier themes of chaos and corruption. When the "October violence" ends, Grace returns to Boca Grande to learn that Charlotte has been shot, her body thrown on the lawn of the American Embassy. Grace can reconstruct the circumstances of her arrest ("*Soy norteamericana*," she told the soldier who knocked the passport from her hand with the butt of his carbine, then, "Don't you lay your fucking hands on me"), but she does not know which side actually ordered her death. Although Charlotte and many others lose their lives to the revolution, the only political change it effects is Victor's replacement by Antonio as Minister of Defense.

The novel closes with a return to the theme of part one, that of history. In the final chapter Grace confesses that, because she had to rely so much on hearsay in telling Charlotte's story, she has not been the biographer–historian she wanted to be. She attests that she is still interested in the past, but understands it no better. Her confession of failure is linked with a deliberate image of obscurity: "Today we are clearing some coastal groves by slash-and-burn and a pall of smoke hangs over Boca Grande. . . . The smoke obscures the light. . . . I wish that I could see the light today." The smoke blocking the "opaque equatorial light" so loved by Grace is our final view of Boca Grande and a symbol of all that Grace does not understand in the life of Charlotte.

Thus Charlotte's story cannot be fully grasped

without considering the complex character of the woman who tells it. On one level Grace is completely reliable; a trained observer of persons and societies, she is entirely objective in her reporting of facts, dialogues and events. Her presentation of Charlotte can be completely trusted; she is right to call Charlotte's story one of delusion, and she analyzes these delusions with insight and precision. On another level, however, Grace is totally unreliable. Because she is morally obtuse, she cannot put together the pieces of Charlotte's story into a coherent whole; she does not know what the story means. The reader can trust Grace's analysis of Charlotte, but to understand Didion's moral vision in the novel, he must analyze Grace, realizing that, while she is an effective scientist, she is inadequate as moral philosopher. To put this distinction another way, Charlotte's delusions are primarily social, whereas Grace's delusions are moral and spiritual.

I will begin my discussion of character with Charlotte rather than Grace for two reasons. First, Charlotte's illusions are typically American, and it is important to understand them because of Didion's profound concern with American values. Second, we need to know Charlotte's story thoroughly in order to see what Grace could not—its universal moral significance.

The tragedy of Charlotte Douglas, like that of Maria Wyeth, resulted because Charlotte lived in a world of delusions, refusing to recognize that the actual world around her did not conform to the values upon which her life was built. Charlotte absorbed traditional American values as a child, but she could not see these critically and objectively because she never examined either herself or her society. As an anthropologist, however, Grace *can* describe Charlotte's childhood with objectivity:

As a child of comfortable family in the temperate zone she had been as a matter of course provided with clean sheets, orthodontia, lamb chops, living grandparents, attentive godparents, one brother named Dickie, ballet lessons, and casual timely information about menstruation and the care of flat silver, as well as a small wooden angel . . . to sit on her bed table and listen to her prayers. In these prayers the child Charlotte routinely asked that "it" turn out all right, "it" being unspecified and all-inclusive, and she had been an adult for some years before the possibility occurred to her that "it" might not.

The passage illustrates many of the values and some of the character traits of the adult Charlotte, who has not changed much from the little girl who prayed to her carved wooden angel. The family, which must consist of parents, grandparents, and (preferably two) children, is the center of life and the source of all good. Clean sheets and orthodontia are roughly equal in value with one's brother. A casual materialism ("the care of flat silver") coexists with blind confidence in a powerful deity who, once appealed to, will resolve all problems with dispatch whether or not they have been clearly articulated. (Characteristically, Charlotte avoided defining her problems, preferring denial to definition.)

Charlotte's need to be part of a functioning family is so powerful that she cannot come to terms with her daughter's renunciation of her, preferring to live in an imaginary past in which she and Marin were "inseparable" (her favorite word). She tells Grace several different versions of a weekend when she and Marin flew to Copenhagen in order to see the colored lights of the Tivoli Gardens. Her most tenacious memory is of an Easter morning when she and Warren took Marin, dressed in a straw hat and a flowered lawn dress, to the Carlyle for lunch—a traditional family celebrating a traditional holiday.

Charlotte leaves Warren when he rejects the traditional role of husband and father, when it becomes apparent that he is an inveterate alcoholic and freeloader. Moving to the West Coast, she marries Leonard Douglas, a successful lawyer who defends political activists and arranges "deals" between leaders of Third World countries.

Living with Leonard and Marin in an elegant house on California Street in San Francisco, Charlotte feels again that she is an integral part of a family. But she sees her daughter as she wishes her to be, as a happy adolescent with a good tennis backhand, a student at Berkeley who spends weekends skiing at Squaw Valley. When the FBI come to the house on California Street to tell her that Marin is wanted for her part in detonating a bomb in the Transamerica Building and hijacking a plane at San Francisco airport, Charlotte "could make no connection between the pitiless revolutionist they described and Marin, who at seven had stood on a chair to make her own breakfast and wept helplessly when asked to clean her closet." Charlotte is so distanced from her daughter's actual life that she is surprised to learn that Marin has not been registered as a student for the past two quarters.

Parenthood is for Charlotte an act of religious devotion; her passport is stamped "occupation: *Madre*," and her extreme dedication to this occupation has led her to set up her own image of her daughter as an idol. Although it is clear to the reader that Marin has only a modest intelligence and very little loyalty to her parents, the religious quality of Charlotte's attitude toward her is captured in Grace's description: "Charlotte believed that when she walked through the valley of the shadow she would be sustained by the taste of Marin's salt tears, her body and blood." Gerardo reports that during Charlotte's interrogation before her execution, she cried not for God, but for Marin.

Despite her marriage to a man who works to implement social and political change, Charlotte denies that such change can affect her life. Yet, through Marin, revolution determines the course of the last two years of her life. In the student uprising of the late sixties Marin aligned herself with the most radical faction, the group using guerrilla tactics in its attempt to destroy the Establishment. In the novel, Didion parallels this uprising to that in Boca Grande, making clear that revolution and violence are not confined to California. In neither revolution is the Establishment destroyed, but both serve to cause several deaths and to separate parent from child: Charlotte loses Marin forever to events of the sixties, and in Boca Grande Grace likes her son less and less as he becomes progressively more involved in the rebellion against his uncle, the defense minister of the country. Whereas Charlotte sees Marin as a child-goddess, however, Grace has no illusions about her son, perceiving him correctly as cold, snobbish, and manipulative.

Living alone in Boca Grande, separated from both her first and second husbands, Charlotte persists in the fantasy that she is part of a family (at different times she tells Grace that she and Leonard are inseparable and that she and Warren are inseparable) and that Marin will find her (for several months she goes to the airport in hopes of meeting her daughter). Charlotte persists in another kind of fantasy, also a legacy from her middle-class childhood: she believes that social ills can be cured, that revolution inevitably means progress, that the spiral of history turns ever upward. These fantasies, which Didion also considers to be typical of Charlotte's generation of middle-class Americans, are based on stubborn, blissful ignorance:

She was immaculate of history, innocent of politics. . . . She understood that something was always going on in the world but believed that it would turn out all right. . . . She . . . associated it [revolution] with events in France and Russia that had probably turned out all right, otherwise why had they happened.

Charlotte has no sooner arrived in Boca Grande than she applies her romantic vision of history to the country, describing it in letters to the *New Yorker* as a "land of contrasts," "the economic fulcrum of the Americas," a country whose very *favelas* embody a "spirit of hope." Grace, who has lived in Boca Grande for several decades and is a trained observer of societies, tells the reader that Boca

Grande, lacking hills, ruins or even waterfalls, offers few contrasts to the eye, that it exports only copra, parrots, anaconda skins, and macramé shawls, and that it has no slums, since rich and poor alike live in cinderblock houses.

Undaunted by Grace's skepticism, Charlotte develops visionary schemes to attract tourists to Boca Grande. She plans a film festival, drawing up lists of names of actors and directors and agents; she plans to convert a dirty storefront into a chic boutique to sell needlepoint canvases of her own design, ignoring the fact that the entire market for such a product would be limited to Grace and her family. Some of her projects, more practical, are partially realized; when an epidemic of cholera breaks out, she gives inoculation for thirty-four hours without sleeping, stopping only when an army colonel seizes the vaccine (supplied by the Red Cross) because she refuses to pay him for it. She volunteers to work in a birth-control clinic, but her effectiveness there is reduced by her persistent advice to women that they should use diaphragms, when the clinic has only intrauterine devices in stock.

Behind Charlotte's activities lies the naive assumption that all other persons share her values and, to some extent, her experience. When Grace points out to her that the diaphragm is not considered a practical method of birth control in underdeveloped countries, Charlotte responds that any woman could learn to use a diaphragm, since she did. When the army colonel seizes the cholera vaccine, she cannot accept his indifference to the people dying of the epidemic and thus concludes that the army must be lending its resources to the innoculation program. Several months after this incident, on one of the few occasions in the novel when Charlotte accepts a painful reality, she is enraged to come upon Antonio using the unopened crates of Lederle vaccine for target practice.

A Book of Common Prayer includes scenes in San Francisco, Beverly Hills, New Orleans, Mérida, Antigua, Guadeloupe, and Boca Grande. In not one of these places is there evidence of successful attempts to cure social ills, of the "generally upward spiral of history" in which Charlotte Douglas believes. The reader also has occasion to observe many families in the privacy of their homes, as Grace traces Charlotte's southward course. Not one of these fits Charlotte's image of the orderly, loving family. When Charlotte visits her brother's family in Hollister, her sister-in-law is hostile to her, and her brother is hostile to his wife. When Charlotte lights a cigarette,

"Richard and I don't smoke," Linda said.
"We don't fuck either," Dickie said.

In New Orleans Morgan and Lucy Fayard taunt each other during a dinner party with references to each other's lovers, and at Christmas dinner in Boca Grande Antonio shatters two porcelain wise men while attempting to shoot a lizard; he then tries to start an argument with his wife, who does not believe in guns; all the while Elena is making veiled references to her brother-in-law's mistresses. The ultimate undermining of family unity occurs in the final section of the novel, when Victor, Boca Grande's defense minister, attempts to kill his brother Antonio, who aspires to Victor's job. In four assassination attempts, Victor fails to kill Antonio, although he kills six other persons and injures fourteen. Thus, when depicting the revolution in Boca Grande, Didion is able to portray both the disintegration of family loyalty and the casual use of violence to the end not of social good but of political power for individuals.

Although the breaking up of traditional institutions is by no means confined to the United States, Didion does consider Charlotte's delusions to be typically North American (especially western) and middle-class and also characteristic of Charlotte's generation (it is clear from the few dates used in the novel that Charlotte was born about

1930). Again and again in the novel Charlotte is referred to as *la norteamericana*; her nationality is, in fact, one of the few stable elements in her identity. Her character is western American not only in its delusions, but also in its odd mixture of physical daring and intellectual weakness. Although her thinking was seldom clear, Charlotte could kill a live chicken by wringing its neck or skin an iguana for stew. Having grown up on a ranch, she retained certain frontier skills that repeatedly startled Grace, who expected physical weakness of a woman so emotionally unstable.

Despite her occasional demonstrations of physical hardiness, Charlotte has no control of her life because she cannot free herself of comfortable illusions. Her first husband, Warren Bogart, another North American, is her equal for romantic illusions, although his take a somewhat different form. Indifferent to material or political concerns, indifferent to family, Warren believes that life should be spent in drinking and sexual gymnastics, both activities that drown reason in bodily ecstasy or numbness. Like Charlotte, he, too, loses control of his life, drifting from one sexual partner to another (preferring two at once, when he can arrange it), counting on Leonard or a cousin or a friend to provide him with food and lodging. Yet for all his infidelity, Warren has a romantic attachment to Charlotte that Didion contrasts with the cold sexuality of Latin American males. "We should do this all our lives," he repeats to her over and over after their ritual hour in bed, and Charlotte cannot resist his blandishments even though she shares him daily with other women who are more often than not the wives or cousins of his friends.

Charlotte and Warren lead disorderly, nomadic lives; Grace and Leonard lead stable, orderly ones. Yet the control that Grace exercises over her life is only temporary, for she will soon die of cancer, the same disease that took Warren's life. Social themes in *A Book of Common*

Prayer shade into spiritual ones, and one of the most prominent of these is the existential theme that we should care
for each other, because in the end we share a common
fate. This theme, like the other universal themes of the
novel, is revealed through the novel's action and
characters; Grace does not articulate it because her own
moral and intellectual limitations prevent her from
perceiving it.

Didion made her narrator blind to certain moral
truths for several reasons. First, she wanted to write a
novel rather than a sermon; thus she preferred that the
truths be implicit within the action rather than explicitly
stated. Also, she achieved fine dramatic irony by creating
a narrator who was herself deluded even while she exposed the delusions of Charlotte. Finally, through the
character of Grace, who practiced both anthropology and
biochemistry, Didion exposed the limitations of a purely
scientific viewpoint. To understand the lack of a moral
dimension in Grace's perception, it is necessary to consider her character and her complex relationship with
Charlotte.

Grace claims that her interest in Charlotte is purely
intellectual: "I am interested in Charlotte Douglas only insofar as she passed through Boca Grande, only insofar as
the meaning of that sojourn continues to elude me." She
tries to reduce her concern for Charlotte to the level of an
intellectual puzzle in order to achieve emotional distance
from her; what she truly feels is not emotional distance,
however, but a maternal concern that is very close to love.
Her relationship with Charlotte begins with simple
neighborly gestures; she visits Charlotte in the Caribe
Hotel when she is ill at Christmas; she sends her
chloromycetin tablets for dysentery when Charlotte has
trouble obtaining them in a drugstore. She is moved to
sympathy for Charlotte when she learns from the
American ambassador the story of Marin's flight; she is
moved to deeper sympathy by Charlotte's compulsive

retelling of past incidents from Marin's childhood that show the (perhaps imagined) closeness of mother and daughter. She tries, gently, to point out to Charlotte that her view of Boca Grande is an idealized one. When the revolution is imminent, she tries desperately to persuade Charlotte to leave the country with her.

Grace does not claim emotional distance from Charlotte on all occasions. When Charlotte realizes that people in Boca Grande died of cholera simply because the army chose to seize the vaccine that could have saved them, Grace confesses, "I loved Charlotte in that moment as a parent loves a child who has just fallen from a bicycle, met a pervert, lost a prize, come up in any way against the hardness of the world." After Charlotte's death Grace's love for her is evident in her behavior. While waiting for the coffin holding her body to be loaded onto the plane leaving for San Francisco, Grace impulsively buys a t-shirt printed like an American flag and drops it on the coffin. A few weeks later Grace travels from Boca Grande to a dirty room in Buffalo, New York, simply to tell Charlotte's daughter that her mother had her always in her mind. Grace never sees, though, that these actions derive from her deep emotional commitment to Charlotte, a commitment that is in fact parallel to Charlotte's commitment to Marin. Rather, she sees these actions as meaningless, telling us that she did not belong in the dirty room in Buffalo, and that the placing of the American flag on Charlotte's coffin was pointless.

Grace sees her own actions and those of Charlotte as meaningless because she is seeking from them a kind of meaning that human behavior simply does not yield. For all of her adult life Grace has wanted to define human behavior and human life in objective, scientific terms. She gave up anthropology when she "stopped believing that observable activity defined anthropos"; she turned to biochemistry in hopes of finding a definition in that microscopic world. But although she learned that certain traits (e.g., fear of the dark) could be synthesized in the laboratory, the discipline of the hard sciences did not yield up a definition of human life any more than the social sciences had. Grace concedes that she could never find "the molecular structure of the protein which defined Charlotte Douglas." But (Didion would say) to expect scientific research of any kind to define either human life in general or individual personality in particular is a kind of arrogance. Science can explain certain phenomena, but it cannot "define" human personality, which remains fundamentally mysterious and unpredictable.

A Book of Common Prayer demonstrates this fundamental mystery through its action and characters. Grace says that her own view of sexual current is mechanical (e.g., explicable by principles of chemistry and physics), but she cannot explain why Charlotte's sexual attractiveness is so powerful that both Gerardo and her brother-in-law decide to seduce her within the first five minutes of meeting her, and Warren Bogart travels across the continent to seduce her once again. Grace tells us that Charlotte and Gerardo reversed the neutron field on her lawn during their first seductive meeting, but this statement does not explain sexual behavior, does not tell us why Charlotte goes to bed with any man who wants her or why she left a responsible husband who cared for her to travel with a man who cared for no one except himself. Grace's view of sexuality is really no more enlightened than that of her aunt, who considered "the marriage bed as the true tropic of fever and disquiet" and advised Grace upon marriage to boil water for douches and avoid playing bridge with depressed acquaintances.

Grace teases herself with all of the inconsistencies in Charlotte's character, seeking scientific explanations for them. Charlotte was afraid to swim in clouded water, yet she saved the life of a man choking on a piece of steak by making an incision in his trachea with a boning knife, an act of courage and intelligence that even her frontier childhood could not account for. Charlotte seemed not to notice when half of the clinic in which she was working was blown away by a bomb; yet she remembered that her underwear was handstitched in the Phillipines rather than the Azores. In her attempt to "define" Charlotte Douglas, Grace is frustrated by the almost infinite complexity of human character.

The first sentence in *A Book of Common Prayer* is Grace's statement, "I will be her witness." Grace used "witness" in the judicial sense; like a character witness at a trial, she wanted to publicly explain and defend Charlotte's behavior with rational principles. The last sentence in the novel is her confession, "I have not been the witness I wanted to be"; she was unable to explain Charlotte's behavior by any principles that she understood and accepted. In fact, Grace served as Charlotte's "witness" in a religious rather than a judicial sense; just as a godparent promises to a child at baptism, she tried to give Charlotte worldly help and protection and to lead her to the truth—in short, to lend her "grace." (To the extent that Charlotte is a modern Christ-figure who idolizes her child rather than a deity, Grace is also witness as an apostle who tells her story). Grace does not realize that she has been this kind of witness because she does not see people or the universe as vested with spiritual qualities, or even with the humane qualities of love and tenderness. Didion does see this, however, and, against the political and familial chaos to which Grace is also witness, Didion suggests a measured hope through the repeated references to the Easter morning when Charlotte, Warren, and Marin constituted, for one day at least, a family.

Although Grace never recognizes the spiritual dimension in Charlotte that Didion suggested with the title of the novel, she does gain some insight into herself in the process of telling Charlotte's story. In chapter 1 she insists upon the simplicity of her own character: "I have been for fifty of my sixty years a student of delusion, a

prudent traveler from Denver, Colorado." She presents
herself as Charlotte's opposite, a clear-sighted, unemo-
tional person who understands herself and others, who
has never been governed by passion or illusion. She
presents her past without detail and without feeling: "My
mother died of influenza one morning when I was eight.
My father died of gunshot wounds, not self-inflicted, one
afternoon when I was ten. From that afternoon until my
sixteenth birthday I lived alone in our suite at the Brown
Palace Hotel. I have lived in equatorial America since
1935 and only twice had fever."

Yet as Grace tells Charlotte's story she discovers that
she shares with Charlotte sorrow, passion, and illusion.
She shares with her, first, the loss of her child. Although
she sees Gerardo often, he is "lost" to her because he
shares none of her values. Over thirty years old, he has
never worked, preferring to ride his Suzuki motorcycle
around Paris or his Alfa Romeo around Boca Grande. He
spends his time in bed with women or playing political
games. Grace tells us, wistfully, "I like him but not too
much anymore." In addition to profound loss, Grace
shares sexual passion with Charlotte, although it has been
banished to her dreams and even there is only hinted at.
After Charlotte's death the manager of her hotel gives
Grace some pages that Charlotte had typed: "On those
pages she had tried only to rid herself of her dreams, and
these dreams seemed to deal only with sexual surrender
and infant death, commonplaces of the female obsessional
life. We all have the same dreams." Finally, Grace shares
with Charlotte illusions about persons close to her. She
thought of her dead husband as a planter of coconut
palms, and never suspected that, like Gerardo, he had
played political games; she is shocked to learn from
Leonard that he was the man who financed the
Tupamaros. On the final page of the novel Grace confesses, "I am less and less certain that this story has been
one of delusion. Unless the delusion was mine."

Although Grace learns that she shares with Charlotte more human frailty than she was aware of, her insight stops short of the ability to generalize about human experience. The novel itself, however, does generalize; it tells us that people are bound together by love and gratitude on the one hand, and by corruption and death on the other. The large square emerald that Charlotte wears in place of a wedding ring serves as a symbol of this bond. At the beginning of the novel we know only that the ring is striking for its size and beauty and that Leonard brought it to Charlotte from "wherever he had gone to meet the man who financed the Tupamaros." At a cocktail party in Boca Grande, Charlotte slides the ring up and down on her finger in a sexually suggestive gesture, as she tells Victor that Boca Grande needs a film festival. When she is arrested during the revolution, she manages to mail the ring to Grace, together with Marin's address. By this time Grace knows that the ring was given to Leonard by her husband Edgar in Bogatá, in payment for Leonard's support of the Tupamaros. After Charlotte's death Grace tries to return the ring to Marin in Buffalo. Thus the ring, itself circular, travels a circular route that connects most of the major characters in the novel, underscoring bonds of love as well as those of venality and mortality.

Mortality, the one experience other than birth that everyone shares, is a prominent theme in the novel. Although the experience of death is common, however, attitudes toward it are almost endlessly various. Charlotte thinks little of death before Marin's disappearance, but after it she is overwhelmed by memories of her parents' deaths. Her own possible death she refuses to contemplate, brushing off Grace's warnings that she could be killed in the revolution. Grace's parents died when she was a child; her attitude toward death is in sharp contrast to Charlotte's:

Unlike Charlotte I learned early to keep death in my line of sight, keep it under surveillance, keep it on cleared ground and away from any brush where it might coil unnoticed.

Warren behaves more outrageously than ever in the face of death, intensifying his drinking and sexual activity, making people as uncomfortable as possible by training his girl friend to recite romantic poems about death by Tennyson and Bryant. "None of you is dying as fast as I'm dying," he tells the Fayards, "which I believe allows me certain privileges." Death does not serve to ennoble any of the characters in the novel; it is simply a potent fact in nature that measures love and friendship and gives urgency to life.

In *A Book of Common Prayer* Didion is making a powerful existential statement: bound together by the certainty of death, living without benefit of belief in a benevolent deity, we can only care for each other. In words that repeat those spoken by Lily in *Run River*, Warren tells Charlotte, "It doesn't matter whether you take care of somebody or somebody takes care of you. . . . It's the same thing in the end." Ironically, Warren makes no effort to care for anyone. Others in the novel do, however. Charlotte cares for her dying baby and for the children who swim in the hotel pool in Boca Grande. Leonard cares for Warren, even to serving as sole mourner at his funeral, and, with certain lapses, he tries to care for Charlotte. Didion lays much stress on the bond between women, a bond formed by common experience: "We all have the same dreams," Grace conceded. When Victor and Antonio bully their wives at a Christmas party, the women comfort each other:

For a moment two of my three sisters-in-law stood . . . and buried their faces in each other's shoulders and stroked each other's hair. Only their silence suggested their tears.

In what is of course the most important example of women bonding, Grace tries to care for Charlotte. Didion sees in all of these attempts both dignity and pathos; the person caring is ennobled, even while the effort fails. It is

precisely because the effort fails so often that Didion gave
her novel its particular title. The reader infers from the
action of the novel that human life is not guided by principles that can be comprehended rationally; since the
book cannot explain the fates that fall to its characters, it
becomes a prayer for all of them, but a prayer to an
elusive and apparently capricious deity.

The prayer, of course, is Didion's; Grace has neither
belief nor interest in any kind of deity. From time to time
her narration seems to mock the rhythms of prayer,
however. Passages employing rhythm and parallel
sentence structure (such as the following, in which Grace
describes Warren Bogart) achieve a liturgical effect
reminiscent of certain psalms:

> His face had been coarsened by self-contempt.
> His mind had been coarsened by self-pity. . . .
> I have noticed that it is never enough to be right.
> I have noticed that it is necessary to be better.

For the most part, however, the narrative voice is
conversational, employing sentence fragments or address-
ing the reader directly, changing its mind:

> Call this my own letter from Boca Grande.
> No. Call it what I said. Call it my witness to Charlotte
> Douglas.

Didion frequently emphasizes ideas by allowing separate sentences or fragments to stand as paragraphs:

> Sexual current.
> The retreat into pastoral imagery to suggest this current has
> always seemed to me curious and decadent.
> The dissolve through the goldenrod.
> The romance of the rose.
> Equally specious.
> As usual I favor a mechanical view.

Although abrupt, choppy passages like this one are
balanced by full-length paragraphs, even the paragraphs

are tight and colloquial, without expansive descriptions or explanations. The succinct style of the novel is characteristic of Didion and appropriate to the blunt, straightforward personality of Grace Strasser-Mendana, her narrator.

A Book of Common Prayer received more immediate public notice than either of Didion's earlier novels, and most of the notice was highly favorable. Peter Prescott of *Newsweek* called it "a remarkably good novel."[2] In her review of the book for *The New York Times Book Review*, Joyce Carol Oates said of Didion, "She has been an articulate witness to the most stubborn and intractable truths of our time, a memorable voice, partly eulogistic, partly despairing, always in control."[3] Reviewers lauded Didion's ability to dramatize the breakdown of contemporary social structures through convincing characterizations such as those of Charlotte Douglas and Warren Bogart. Although few reviewers seemed to recognize the limitations in Grace's view of Charlotte, the character of Grace was equally acclaimed.

Didion's prose style in the novel earned responses ranging from extravagant praise to mocking parody. Benjamin Stein in the *National Review* acclaimed the book as "an exquisite, magnificant, breathtaking piece of fiction . . . I cannot think of a living writer whose prose matches Miss Didion's level of simple elegance or the tremendous lyricism of [certain] passages."[4] Susan Lardner, on the other hand, wrote her contemptuous review for *The New Yorker* in a style parodying that of the novel.[5] A balanced response to Didion's style was that of Frederic Raphael in *Saturday Review*, who allowed that its terseness is occasionally excessive, but affirmed that "under the pared phrases one senses the quick of desire for something more noble, more tender, and more enduring than crass contemporary realism . . . How her work conveys this sense of tragic regret I cannot quite say, but that is exactly why she is an artist."[6] Didion conveys the tenderness, even nobility, of which persons are capable through the actions of Grace Strasser-Mendana; she expresses a "sense of tragic regret" through the vast chasm between the reality of lives like Warren Bogart's and the moral ideals that inform the novel.

Like *A Book of Common Prayer, Slouching Towards Bethlehem*, Didion's first collection of prose essays, is concerned with the chaotic decade of the sixties in America. Turning now to this collection, we shall find Didion's sense of regret quite explicitly rendered, regret not simply for a few individuals, but for an entire nation that seems to have lost its way.

5

Slouching Towards Bethlehem

In the preface to *Slouching Towards Bethlehem*, the collection of essays published in 1968, Didion reviews her liabilities and her assets as a reporter:

I am bad at interviewing people. . . . I do not like to make telephone calls, and would not like to count the mornings I have sat on some Best Western motel bed somewhere and tried to force myself to put through the call to the assistant district attorney. My only advantage as a reporter is that I am so physically small, so temperamentally unobtrusive, and so neurotically inarticulate that people tend to forget that my presence runs counter to their best interests. And it always does.

The reporting role forces Didion to wage a ceaseless battle with shyness; furthermore, she feels guilty after she has written about someone. Why, one wonders, does she engage in the role? One obvious reason is that she was not sufficiently established as a writer of fiction to make a living at that calling before the publication of *Play It As It Lays* in 1970. But, as she herself has pointed out, there are easier ways of making a living. (In "Why I Write" she suggests alchemy as one.) The far deeper reason is her strongly felt need not only to understand the social and political currents that swirl around us all, but also to become immersed in these currents long enough to experience them emotionally as well as intellectually. Behind this need lies her conviction that the individual is shaped by his society; she must therefore confront the social and political reality of contemporary America in order to understand herself. Only as a reporter could she have known Joan Baez, John Wayne, Lucille Miller, the hippies and the police of Haight-Ashbury; knowing these people enabled her to understand the sixties in the United States—and herself—as she could not otherwise have done.

Didion never writes simple news stories, collections of facts arranged in chronological order; rather, she selects and arranges facts to suggest larger moral issues or reflects upon them to make these issues explicit. She has all the qualities essential for excellence in this journalistic tradition: the eye for significant detail, the ear for dialogue, the relentlessly independent mind.

Not all of Didion's essays belong in the tradition of journalism, however; many derive from the literary tradi- tion of the informal essay, a tradition that gave birth to the first newspapers in the Western world. The informal essay, while sister to the feature article, is by no means its twin, for a writer may create an informal essay without witnessing any newsworthy events or interviewing a single human being. The subject of the informal essay, whether social or philosophical, derives from the conduct of ordinary life; the first practitioner of the form, the Frenchman Montaigne, wrote his *Essais* after he had retired from active life to devote himself to secluded study and reflection.

The informal or personal essay was born with Montaigne in 1580 in a publication opening with the statement, "C'est moi que je peins" ("It is myself whom I portray").[1] He selected the title *Essais*, which means "at- tempts," to distinguish his work from formal philosophical writings that employ a rigorous logical structure in treating a subject exhaustively. The personal essay is briefer than the formal essay, more succinct, often witty, often rambling in structure. In saying that his essays were about himself, Montaigne referred to the universal rather than the idiosyncratic aspect of the "self"—in fact most of his essays deal with ethical or philosophical subjects. As we will see, Didion in her personal essays often uses her "self" in this manner, as both illustration of and authority for her ideas.

Probably the modern essayist with whom Didion may be most readily compared is George Orwell. They both wrote against stereotyped thinking, received opinion on any subject of importance; they both defined unpleasant truths in areas where pleasant lies prevailed. Although less ideological than Orwell, Didion might be called, as Pritchett called Orwell, "the conscience of his [her] generation." They each developed from their early teen-age years the habit of observing the smallest concrete detail; they each conveyed abstract truths through the description of concretely rendered actions and scenes. When invited to address the faculty of Berkeley, Didion took the title of her talk, "Why I Write," from an essay by Orwell. Like Orwell, Didion views writing as an assertive, even aggressive act in which the writer attempts to impose his will on the reader. The two writers share a certain similarity of style, too; like Orwell, Didion writes clear, crisp prose that favors short Anglo-Saxon words over long or Latinate ones.

As we would expect, there is a distinct difference between the style of Didion's journalism and that of her personal essays. The former relies more on dialogue and carefully observed detail, while her personal essays employ more literary allusion and figurative language. Chapter six will contain an analysis of the most prominent rhetorical and stylistic features of Didion's nonfiction prose. Suffice it to say here that the impression of simplicity that her writings convey is, in fact, a product of highly artful manipulation of language.

Slouching Towards Bethlehem includes twenty essays arranged in three sections: the first section consists of eight feature articles written in the tradition of journalism; the second consists of five personal essays; and the final section comprises seven pieces in which the two traditions are fused. The dominant themes of the collection are those that figure centrally in all three of Didion's novels: the attempt to integrate the past and the present and the contrast between the real and the ideal.

In the eight feature articles that constitute the first section of the book these themes are developed on the level of the community and the nation; in the second section Didion looks for continuity between her own past and present and defines certain of her own ideals. The themes are also found in the book's final section, in which Didion compares the past and the present of particular places.

As we examine the book's individual essays, we will find other themes darting in and out, some social and some philosophical: Is there an American character? If so, what traits form its core? Who are our heroes, and what does our admiration for them mean? How much control does one have over his own actions? As passages from different essays echo and balance each other, the organization of essays within the book gives us point and counterpoint in a thematic richness that would be easily missed were they not collected in a single volume. Thus, despite its time span (1961–1968) and diversity of topic, the book has an inner coherence that reveals the abiding concerns of its author.

The first section of *Slouching Towards Bethlehem*, entitled "Life Styles in the Golden Land," consists of eight articles (all written between 1965 and 1967, and all but one published in *The Saturday Evening Post*) on contemporary persons and events. Although the events occur in California, few of the principal actors were originally Californian, and we soon see that her native state represents for Didion an emblem of the entire country. Considered together, these essays measure the world we have now against the world we once had (or think we had) and have lost.

The first article in this section, "Some Dreamers of

the Golden Dream," concerns a rather sad and shabby
piece of the world we have. The San Bernardino Valley,
originally settled by Mormons, is now lower-middle-class
Protestant—ethnically Protestant, that is, for the culture
appears barren of religious values:

This is the country in which a belief in the literal interpretation
of Genesis has slipped imperceptibly into a belief in the literal interpretation of *Double Indemnity*, the country of the teased hair
and the Capris and the girls for whom all life's promise comes
down to a waltz-length white wedding dress and the birth of a
Kimberly or a Sherry or a Debbi and a Tijuana divorce and a
return to hairdressers' school.

Lucille Miller, the principal dreamer in the story,
came to California from the state of Washington, where
her parents, both Seventh-Day Adventists, taught at
Walla Walla College. Lucille dropped out of Walla Walla
College in 1949 to marry Gordon Miller, another
Seventh-Day Adventist who had graduated from the
University of Oregon dental school. By the summer of
1964 the Millers' lives, viewed from the outside, seemed
serene and settled: "They had achieved the bigger house
on the better street . . . the three children for the
Christmas card, the picture window, the family room, the
newspaper photographs that showed 'Mrs. Gordon
Miller, Ontario Heart Fund Chairman. . . . '" But in fact
their lives were anything but serene. In April Miller
learned that his wife was having an affair with Arthwell
Hayton, their close friend and a prominent San Bernardino lawyer. In May Miller was hospitalized briefly
with a bleeding ulcer and threatened suicide to his friends.
He worried constantly about their debts—over $63,000
that summer. In July Lucille filed for divorce. After seeing a marriage counselor, however, they seemed recon-
ciled and even talked about having a fourth child.

Gordon Miller died in a fire in his Volkswagen on
October 7, 1964. Lucille, who had been with him in the

car, was arrested and charged with murder the next day. At her trial the prosecution claimed that she set the fire, hoping to make the murder appear an accident in order to collect not only his $80,000 in life insurance, but another $40,000 in double indemnity policies. Arthwell Hayton, summoned to testify, did not deny the affair with Mrs. Miller, but persistently denied that there was on his side any "romance" whatsoever. Yet he had written her notes with all the clichés of romance: "Hi Sweetie Pie! You are my cup of tea!! Happy Birthday—you don't look a day over 29!! Your baby, Arthwell."

The breakup of the affair, recorded on tapes Lucille had planted in her car, was more dramatic than the affair itself. When Hayton told her that he did not intend to see her again, she responded, "Look, Sonny Boy, if you think your reputation is going to be ruined, your life won't be worth two cents." He in turn threatened to tell the sheriff a few things about her. As Didion comments, "For an affair between a Seventh-Day Adventist dentist's wife and a Seventh-Day Adventist personal-injury lawyer, it seems a curious kind of dialogue."

Didion cannot be certain that Lucille murdered her husband (she was convicted of first-degree murder by the jury), but she is less concerned with the question of criminal guilt than with the specter of lives without integrity or continuity. Lucille's love for Hayton turns overnight to hate. Hayton himself, forgetting the motel rendezvous and the birthday cards, marries his children's governess seven months after the trial. The San Bernardino women who return to hairdressers' school after their divorces carelessly dismiss their marriages, "'We were just crazy kids,' they say without regret." Didion closes the article with the implicit suggestion that the past cannot so easily be laid aside; Hayton's bride, she reports, wore an "illusion veil" with her long white dress.

Certain fleeting images in the article reappear in subsequent essays, where they are developed in more detail; these links serve to add shades of meaning to "Some Dreamers of the Golden Dream" and to enrich the texture of the entire collection. The Santa Ana winds that blew on the day that Miller's Volkswagen burned are the subject of an entire essay in "Los Angeles Notebook." Reading Didion's discussion of the impact of these winds on individual behavior, we wonder about Lucille Miller's freedom of will on October 7, 1964. The Second Coming, which Didion alludes to as one of the beliefs held by Seventh-Day Adventists, is the title of the Yeats poem quoted at length in the beginning of the book. Certain lines from the poem ("The blood-dimmed tide is loosed, and everywhere/The ceremony of innocence is drowned . . . ") may be taken as comment on the moral chaos in which Lucille Miller and Arthwell Hayton lived their lives.

In marked contrast to the shifting and unstable commitments of Miller and Hayton, the man to whom the next article is dedicated remained constant and predictable all his life. In "John Wayne: A Love Song" Didion describes a man who never claimed he could act, but didn't need to, since his own character, projected and magnified on the screen, became a part of the Golden Dream. Didion fell in love with John Wayne when, as a little girl, she spent an entire summer watching movies like *War of the Wildcats*. It did not seem possible to her, twenty years later, that this man of invincible courage and quiet authority could fall victim to cancer. Coming out of the hospital, Wayne claimed to have "licked the Big C," but Didion sensed that "this would be the one unpredictable confrontation, the one shoot-out Wayne could lose." When asked to interview him on location for his 165th picture, *The Sons of Katie Elder*, she accepted reluctantly, for she would have preferred to keep her dream intact.

What Didion discovered on the set outside Mexico City was that Wayne was in his character and attitudes still the man in the legend. Amidst the idle chatter of his colleagues he spoke seldom, but always with authority. When the young boy on the set received his own chair, he turned shyly to Wayne. "'You see that?' . . . Wayne gave him the smile, the nod, the final accolade. 'I saw it, kid.'" He had a heavy cold, though, and a racking cough; by late afternoon he was often so tired that he needed an oxygen inhalator to complete the day's shooting.

Fifty-seven years old, Wayne denied that he was sick; invoking his personal code, which dictated self-possession, he expressed contempt for a reporter who had drunk too much to walk unattended to his room. But Didion felt that the dream shaped by the legend was gone, whether eroded by time or devoured by cancer. From the dozens of Wayne pictures she saw as a child Didion recognized an ideal world that rewarded courage and individual responsibility, a world "where a man could move free, make his own code and live by it; a world in which, if a man did what he had to do, he could one day take the girl and go riding through the draw and find himself . . . at the bend in the bright river, the cottonwoods shimmering in the early morning sun."

It is of course a frontier dream, a vision of absolute physical freedom and self-reliance, and it is identical with the idealized version of the founding of Sacramento taught to Didion as a child. She concedes that this world may never have existed, but even as an idealized vision it serves to show up the shabby materialism and the failure of character in the present world of Arthwell Haytons and Lucille Millers.

The essay on Wayne is closely linked with another in the first section of the book, "7000 Romaine," an article explaining the appeal of another American folk hero, Howard Hughes. Hughes was hardly lovable and was certainly not available to be interviewed, but Didion demonstrates several parallels between the Hughes myth and the Wayne legend. Although Hughes had neither physical daring nor public presence, he had "absolute personal freedom, mobility, privacy." Didion believes that it was for these frontier virtues, and not for his money and power, that he became a folk hero. She does not consider Americans to be truly materialistic: "Americans are uneasy with their possessions, guilty about power, all of which is difficult for Europeans to perceive because they are themselves so truly materialistic, so versed in the uses of power."

In our fascination with Howard Hughes Didion sees reflected a profound conflict in the American character. She quotes Lionel Trilling, who points out that while "our educated class has . . . a belief in progress, science, social legislation, planning and international cooperation . . . not a single first-rate writer has emerged to deal with these ideas, and the emotions that are consonant with them, in a great literary way." This quotation forms a natural introduction to the two essays in *Slouching* in which Didion does deal with these ideas in a "literary way."

"Where the Kissing Never Stops" and "California Dreaming" describe institutions erected in the service of social ideals. The first, the Institute for the Study of Nonviolence, is a small school in the Carmel Valley owned by Joan Baez; the second, the Center for the Study of Democratic Institutions, is a retreat in the Santa Barbara hills originally funded by the Ford Foundation. Didion discovers many contrasts between the two, but surprisingly, they offer also many similarities. Joan Baez, the folksinger whose first album made her both rich and famous, is a college dropout who began the school because she herself felt the need to learn what the world's great minds had thought about nonviolence; Robert M. Hutchins, president of the Center for the Study of Democratic Institutions, was formerly president of the University of Chicago and remains one of the country's foremost educators. The Institute for the Study of Nonviolence operates by accepting, on a first-come basis, fifteen students who pay $120 for a six-week session during which they do ballet exercises to Beatles records and discuss their reading: Gandhi, Thoreau, C. Wright Mills, and Marshall McLuhan. The Center for the Study of Democratic Institutions operates by inviting experts to discussions on broad topics such as "The City" or "The Emerging Constitution." Discussions are taped, and papers read are published and widely disseminated.

Didion characterizes each of these institutions by the dramatic method of simply describing what she sees and hears. At Joan Baez' school the participants, who are very young, debate whether or not the Vietnam Day Committee at Berkeley was wise to discuss the issues with Hell's Angels "on the hip level."

"O.K.," someone argues. "So the Angels just shrug and say 'our thing's violence.' How can the V.D.C. guy answer that?"

They discuss a proposal from Berkeley for an International Nonviolent Army: "The idea is, we go to Vietnam and we go into these villages, and then if they burn them, we burn too."

"It has a beautiful simplicity," someone says.

It is hard to imagine a more naive discussion than this one—except possibly the following, heard by Didion at the prestigious Center for the Study of Democratic Institutions:

"Don't make the mistake of taking a chair at the big table," I was warned *sotto voce* on my first visit to the Center. "The talk there is pretty high-powered."

"Is there any evidence that living in a violent age encourages violence?" someone was asking at the big table.

"That's hard to measure."

"I think it's the Westerns on television."

"I tend [pause] to agree."

The most striking difference that Didion perceives between the two institutes is that, whereas Baez is completely candid in her admission of both confusion and ignorance, Hutchins' Center is pretentious and self-satisfied "in its conviction that everything said around the place mystically improves the national, and in fact the international, weal."

Baez' Institute and Hutchins' Center are the contemporary equivalent of churches; they exist for the study and worship, not of God, but of "nonviolence" and "democracy." If Hutchins is a bishop of the new religion, then Baez is a saint whose most striking characteristics, Didion notes, are "her absolute directness, her absence of guile." She cares little for money, having turned down innumerable offers for concerts; her most ardent desire is to move people. Ironically, she can do so most successfully through music. Although her friendliness is touching, her intellect is neither trained nor naturally powerful. Because her approach to politics is "instinctive, pragmatic," her political beliefs are hopelessly vague. "Frankly, I'm down on communism," she tells Didion.

This confession of a negative attitude toward communism may explain why Didion followed her essay on Baez with one entitled "Comrade Laski, C.P.U.S.A. (M.-L.)" Michael Laski was General Secretary of the Central Committee of the Communist Party U.S.A. (Marxist-Leninist), a passionate twenty-six-year-old revolutionary from Brooklyn who dropped out of U.C.L.A. and was spending his time at the Workers International Bookstore in Watts, the West Coast headquarters of the splinter group of the Communist Party to which he belonged. Having rejected the traditional American Communist Party and the Progressive Labor Party for various flaws of doctrine, Laski was seen by Didion as a rigid, lonely idealist.

What is remarkable about this brief essay is the way in which Didion reveals the young man to the reader through dialogue and gesture: "He had with him a small red book of Mao's poems, and as he talked he squared it on the table, aligned it with the table edge first vertically and then horizontally." His fanaticism stands in sharp contrast to the relaxed cheerfulness of Baez, who is approximately his age—in the last glimpse we are given of that young woman, she is eating potato salad from a bowl with her fingers. It seems inevitable that Laski should be eagerly awaiting the same violent revolution that Baez hopes to avert.

"Marrying Absurd" seems at first glance a rather frivolous essay; everyone knows, after all, that one can marry fast and cheaply in Las Vegas. As she often does, however, Didion has buried in the essay a thesis paragraph that casts a richer, deeper light over the entire piece:

Las Vegas is the most extreme and allegorical of American settlements, bizarre and beautiful in its venality and in its devotion to immediate gratification, a place the tone of which is set by mobsters and call girls and ladies' room attendants with amyl nitrate poppers in their uniform pockets. Almost everyone notes that there is no "time" in Las Vegas, no night and no day and no past and no future. . . . One is standing on a highway in the middle of a vast hostile desert looking at an eighty-foot sign which blinks "Stardust" or "Caesar's Palace."

Given these surroundings, one would expect couples marrying in Las Vegas to be acting on impulse, eloping or fleeing parental prohibition. But such is not the case: many couples *plan* to marry in one of the nineteen chapels that advertise "Sincere and Dignified Since 1954." They come with their parents, "the bride in a veil and white satin pumps, the bridegroom usually in a white dinner jacket, and even an attendant or two, a sister or a best friend in hot-pink *peau de soie*, a flirtation veil, a carnation nosegay." These are the people whom we pity, for they yearn after tradition without understanding that it is not a package which can be bought, but a tall tree that requires time and fertile soil in which to grow roots. Their marriage is "absurd" not because it is impulsive, but because it is a traditional ceremony occurring in a place barren of tradition, a no-man's-land that recognizes neither past nor future.

The theme of rootlessness, of life without sense of time or place, is continued in "Slouching Towards Bethlehem," the title piece and the longest essay in the collection. "Slouching Towards Bethlehem" is a major document in social history of the sixties, both a dramatization and an analysis of the hippie movement in the United States. "Hippie" was the term somewhat vaguely assigned to alienated young people who dropped out of school or work and drifted to Haight-Ashbury in San Francisco, where they had access to drugs and could live cheaply. Conservative Americans condemned them as irresponsible, while many liberal thinkers regarded them as both victims and critics of our competitive, militaristic society.

To gather material for "Slouching Towards Bethlehem" Didion did not simply drive through the district and do street-corner interviews; she looked up "contacts" and spent long periods of time with the young people where they lived—in one case a rather pleasant apartment, in another the garage of a condemned hotel. She came to know about half a dozen hippies; she also met with psychiatrists, the police, and a self-appointed social worker trying to start a VISTA program in the district. For the most part she simply observed and listened, forbearing to judge.

The leading characters in her drama include Deadeye, a former Hell's Angel who wants to set up a "groovy religious group—Teenage Evangelism"; Gerry, Deadeye's "old lady," a large, hearty girl who dropped out of the University of Washington and now writes childish romantic poetry; Sue Ann, a pale girl, the mother of a three-year-old child, who spends her time cooking seaweed or baking macrobiotic bread; Steve, a young painter who announces that he lost love on acid but found it on grass; and Max, a young man in his twenties, fugitive from Eastern schools and clinics, who claims that he lives "free of all the old middle-class Freudian hang-ups."

Didion's drama is circular and fragmented, like the lives of its actors; characters appear briefly, disappear, and reappear several days later. On her first day in the district she meets a boy looking for a ride to New York; when she runs into him in Golden Gate Park a few days later he tells her, "I hear New York's a bummer." The first time she visits Deadeye's apartment there is a girl sleeping on the floor; when she returns a week later the girl is in the same place. The next day Gerry tells her casually that the girl has been hospitalized with pneumonia.

The climax of "Slouching Towards Bethlehem" is the reader's realization that all of the hippies are emotionally stunted; they are essentially children playing at being grown-ups. They fulfill their most elemental needs—for food, companionship, and sexual release—but they avoid all the complexities of adult life: the need to find work that is rewarding and productive, the enduring commitment to another person, the search for words to communicate profound and intricate feeling. They do not rebel against the conventions of society; they ape them, just as children do. The women do all the cooking and cleaning: Sharon defines washing dishes as an aesthetic act, "I mean you watch that blue detergent blob run on the plate, watch the grease cut—well, it can be a real trip." The men propound visionary schemes: "What I want to do now," Deadeye tells Didion, "is set up a house where a person of any age can come, spend a few days, talk over his problems." Lacking initiative, discipline, and the adult capacity to postpone gratification, however, they cannot begin to implement any of their ideas.

Their dependence on drugs is a form of regression, a search for the dependence and total passivity of childhood. Didion is present during a communal "trip" on LSD:

At three-thirty that afternoon Max, Tom, and Sharon placed tabs under their tongues and sat down together in the living room to wait for the flash. Barbara stayed in the bedroom, smoking hash. During the next four hours a window banged once in Barbara's room, and about five-thirty some children had a fight on the street. A curtain billowed in the afternoon wind. A cat scratched a beagle in Sharon's lap. Except for the sitar music on the stereo there was no other sound or movement until seven-thirty, when Max said "Wow."

Most of their favorite words—"wow" and "groovy"—have little meaningful content. Their topics of conversation (food, sex, and drugs) are primitive; even money is called by a term that refers to its most elemental meaning, the power to purchase food: "bread." Most people become articulate because they need words to integrate their past into their present, and to struggle with both present feelings and future plans. These young people have turned their backs on the struggle through which one becomes an adult; thus they have no need for words to shape understanding, to define themselves as individuals.

The older generation must bear some responsibility for their infantile character. "These were children who grew up cut loose from the web of cousins and great-aunts and family doctors and lifelong neighbors who had traditionally suggested and enforced the society's values." The police whom Didion meets in Haight-Ashbury do not understand them; Officer Gerrans, who was responsible for more "busts" than any other policeman, first tells Didion that the problems in the district are "juveniles and narcotics," then, after consulting with his superior, confiscates her notes. More surprising, the many reporters and photographers whom Didion meets in the district understand no better than the policemen. They were determined to assign the "hippie movement" some meaning in history, whether "artistic avant-garde" or "thoughtful protest"; they failed to see that these children were living without memory or plans, outside of time.

The hippies are the "falcon" in Yeats' poem, turning

dizzily, unable to hear the "falconer," a guiding voice capable of lending purpose to their lives. Didion sees them as a symptom of deep disorder in the society as a whole; she believes that because of the absence of coherent values among the older generation, no enduring values have been transmitted to the younger:

We were seeing the desperate attempt of a handful of patheti-cally unequipped children to create a community in a social vacuum. Once we had seen these children, we could no longer overlook the vacuum, no longer pretend that the society's atomization could be reversed.

Didion rarely allows herself such direct commentary in this essay; for the most part its themes are conveyed through carefully selected bits of dialogue, ironic jux-taposition of vignettes, and scrupulously observed detail. Her essentially dramatic method reveals the profound ig-norance and childish passivity of the hippies with an economy and subtlety of impact that interpretative analy-sis could not possibly achieve.

The next section in *Slouching Towards Bethlehem*, en-titled "Personals," consists of five essays published be-tween 1961 and 1967 in *Vogue, Holiday, The American Scholar* and *The Saturday Evening Post*. As personal essays they of course differ profoundly in form and style from the journalistic essays in the first section. Yet they continue the themes of that section, refining and developing them with a clarity that sheds further light on the earlier essays. Just as Didion was concerned with continuity in our na-tional character, so does she attempt in these essays to in-tegrate her own past and present, both her past and pres-ent "worlds" and her past and present "selves." In the two essays on abstract topics, "On Self-Respect" and "On Morality," moral values that were implicit in her fiction and journalism are illustrated and made explicit.

"On Keeping a Notebook" seems at first to be written in a minor key, a writer poking fun at her own idiosyn-cratic habit of cryptic entries in a notebook, snatches of scenes or conversations which can, if memory serves, recall entire scenarios years later. But the piece is both more serious and more dramatic than the first six pages would seem to indicate. The essay opens with this brief entry from Didion's notebook: "'That woman Estelle . . . is partly the reason why George Sharp and I are separated today.' Dirty crepe-de-Chine wrapper, hotel bar, Wilmington RR, 9:45 a.m. August Monday morning." After studying the notebook for some time, Didion remembers the entire scene: not only the woman in the dirty wrapper, but the bartender mopping the floor, and another woman sitting at the other end of the bar with a man beside her, wearing a plaid silk dress with the hem coming down. She assigns feelings and fantasies to the other woman: she must leave the man and go back to New York City, where she has a luncheon appointment; she sees ahead the "viscous summer sidewalks and the 3 a.m. long-distance calls" and feels mildly sorry for herself.

Not until several pages later does Didion disclose that she was the woman in the plaid silk dress. The disclosure is made in support of the central idea of the essay: although her notebook seems to consist of random observations on facts and other people, its actual subject is herself. Each concrete image or bit of dialogue recorded is in fact shorthand for the complex network of events and feelings that compose the "self" at any given moment. "He was born the night the Titanic went down" is a line spoken by a woman about her husband. Didion lunched with the woman on the terrace of her elegant home, but she drank too much wine and when a checkout clerk in the supermarket later that day spoke about a baby, she felt piercing envy because she wanted a baby and an elegant house by the sea, and had neither.

While admitting that both her method and her memory have their limitations, Didion is making an important point: " . . . we are well advised to keep on nodding terms with the people we used to be, whether we find them attractive company or not." Recalling one's past with precision and objectivity is not egotism, but an exercise in self-knowledge, for all our past selves lie behind our present self, and if we distort or reject these selves we shatter the continuity of our lives.

While integrating one's past and present "selves" is no easy matter, one at least feels that positive growth has occurred, that the present self is an improvement upon the former, less mature person that one was. Changing one's world does not offer a parallel consolation, however. In "On Going Home" Didion confronts the world of her past, questions its relationship with her present, and, through the symbolic event of her daughter's first birthday, wonders about a future she cannot anticipate.

The word "home" itself is ambiguous in this essay. Didion's present home (the essay was written in 1967) is Los Angeles, but she thinks of her parents' house in the Sacramento Valley as home. The two worlds are so far apart that her husband and parents might be speaking a different language. Her brother cannot understand the inability of her husband (an Easterner) to appreciate the advantages of the real-estate transaction known as sale-leaseback, while her husband does not understand that "when we talk about sale-leasebacks and right-of-way condemnations we are talking in code about the things we like best, the yellow fields and the cottonwoods and the rivers rising and falling . . . "

Didion felt both guilt and loss at leaving the rural, insular society to which her parents belonged:

I had by all objective accounts a "normal" and a "happy" family situation, and yet I was almost thirty years old before I could talk to my family on the telephone without crying after I had hung up. . . . Some nameless anxiety colored the emotional charges between me and the place that I came from. The question of whether or not you could go home again was a very real part of the . . . baggage with which we left home in the fifties.

Born in the thirties, Didion grew up in Sacramento before the arrival of either television or industry, phenomena which served to link that agricultural community with the larger society. By the time she arrived in New York City after graduation from Berkeley she must have felt herself light-years away from the quiet town of Sacramento; it is hardly surprising that such profound distance produced "nameless anxiety."

Only a personal bond with her family could bridge the chasm, and Didion seems to have forged that bond. She drives with her father to a ranch he has bought and has a companionable cup of coffee with her mother. Her connection with the past has attenuated (her great-aunts no longer recognize her), but her bond with her parents is firm and her stake in the future, represented by her daughter, is high: "I would like to promise her that she will grow up with a sense of her cousins and of rivers and of her great-grandmother's teacups, . . . but we live differently now and I can promise her nothing like that. I give her a xylophone and a sundress from Madeira, and promise to tell her a funny story."

"On Self-Respect" offers a fresh view of an old subject. We earn self-respect, Didion believes, not by following a particular standard of behavior, but by facing squarely what we are doing and where it is likely to lead. "There is a common superstition that self-respect is a kind of charm against snakes, something that keeps those who have it . . . out of strange beds, ambivalent conversations, and trouble in general. It does not at all. It has nothing to do with the face of things, but concerns instead a separate peace, a private reconciliation."

Didion's concept of self-respect is based upon her conviction that we must arrive at a "separate peace," because at one level of consciousness we truly know ourselves and our motives: "Most of our platitudes not withstanding, self-deception remains the most difficult deception. The tricks that work on others count for nothing in that very well-lit back alley where one keeps assignations with oneself: no winning smiles will do here, no prettily drawn list of good intentions."

The essay is not entirely consistent: Didion's contention that self-respect depends on discipline, "doing things one does not particularly want to do," contradicts her earlier assertion that self-respect has nothing to do with a particular mode of behavior. Also, if this kind of discipline is necessary to self-respect, then Didion's choice of Jordon Baker from *The Great Gatsby* as an exemplar of self-respect is puzzling; Jordon Baker always did precisely what she wanted to do, and frequently lied about it afterward.

Its single logical flaw aside, the essay is stunning in its rhetorical effects and its insight into the disastrous consequences of the absence of self-respect:

> If we do not respect ourselves, we are on the one hand forced to despise those who have so few resources as to consort with us, so little perception as to remain blind to our fatal weaknesses. On the other, we are particularly in thrall to everyone we see, curiously determined to live out—since our self-image is untenable—their false notions of us. . . . Of course I will play Francesca to your Paolo, Helen Keller to anyone's Anna Sullivan: no expectation is too misplaced, no role too ludicrous.

"On Self-Respect" displays a range of literary allusion and a depth of worldly wisdom that suggest a vast experience of life—how remarkable that it was written by a young woman who was twenty-six years old!

The concept of taking responsibility for one's own life that Didion stresses in her essay "On Self-Respect" is expanded to encompass the notion of responsibility to others in another personal essay in this section. In 1967, at a time when intellectuals across the country were condemning America's role in the Vietnam war as immoral, *The American Scholar* invited Didion to write a piece on morality. While never mentioning the war, "On Morality" expresses Didion's firm conviction of the dangers of using the language of moral judgment to describe a political position. The danger resides in the too easy transition from thinking that one's position is moral to thinking that, because it is moral, it can be imposed on everyone. The most monstrous acts in history, she argues, have been perpetrated by persons following their consciences, persons convinced that their views were moral.

In a portion of the essay that bears directly upon her fiction, Didion defines the sphere to which the term "moral" may appropriately be applied—that of individual human relationships. The term describes, first, our fundamental responsibility to a primitive social code that dictates certain obligations (e.g., we bury our dead; we do not leave even the corpse of a stranger on the desert to be devoured by coyotes.) The term also describes our loyalty and commitment to those we love. Didion defines here the moral values we saw embedded in her fiction: the world of Maria Wyeth was immoral because of the failure of loyalty on the part of those who should have loved her; Grace Strasser-Mendana was acting morally both when she condemned the treachery of her brothers-in-law and when she tried to protect Charlotte. Didion considers virtue to be a concrete quality manifesting itself in specific individual actions: "We have no way of knowing—beyond that fundamental loyalty to the social code—what is right and what is wrong, what is good and what is evil."

The essays in the final section of *Slouching Towards Bethlehem*, "Seven Places of the Mind," combine the traditions of journalism with the personal essay. In each essay the place itself is objectively described, while Didion's response to it is frankly personal. In "Notes from a Native Daughter" Didion gives us two views of Sacramento, and then raises the question, which is real? She first depicts the old Sacramento Valley with its beautiful sprawling land and its tiny ugly towns, their sidewalks cracking and paint peeling off the old frame houses. She then presents the new Sacramento of shopping centers and tract houses; at its heart is Aerojet-General, the company that makes parts for rockets and space capsules, a fitting symbol of our technological world. Although the two societies now exist side by side, apparently oblivious to each other, it is abundantly clear to the reader, as it is to Didion, that only one of them will long endure. At the end of the essay she wonders whether it is the old Sacramento or her own irretrievable childhood that she mourns.

Seldom does Didion perceive a place as that place sees itself. In "Letter from Paradise" Didion reports on Hawaii past and present: she takes the tour of Pearl Harbor, crying at the *Arizona* (a ship sunk with 1,102 men aboard and considered by the navy to be still in commission); she visits the National Memorial Cemetery of the Pacific, a vast crater above Honolulu where 19,000 people, many of them boys who never reached their twentieth birthday, lie buried; she visits Hotel Street, where many of the 3,500 Marines on the way to Vietnam, as well as the soldiers and sailors permanently stationed in Hawaii, are getting drunk or getting tattooed. Travel posters to the contrary, Hawaii is not paradise, but a place whose economy is based upon the military and whose memory is dominated by war. Her sojourn there was not the vacation her family anticipated when they sent her off, but it was an ironically appropriate place for one who had been "tired too long and quarrelsome too much."

In many of the essays in this section Didion is an archeologist of American history, reconstructing the past from its architectural relics. She likes Alcatraz ("Rock of Ages"), legendary prison of Al Capone and the Bird Man, now abandoned and overgrown with nasturtiums and geraniums. Men had to confront the reality of their lives here, for there was no escape from the island washed by the cold tide. Didion feels peace in this "ruin devoid of human vanities, clean of human illusions," and perhaps even discovers a hope of salvation for its former notorious inhabitants in the yellowed program from an Easter service that she finds in an empty cell.

In an irony that must have passed unnoticed until Didion collected her essays, while she saw Alcatraz as a sanctuary, she saw the mansions in Newport, Rhode Island, as former prisons—vast, ugly follies in which women were condemned to endless "production—of luncheons, of masked balls, of *marrons glaces*." Against the prevailing view that the wealthy Easterner in mid-nineteenth century America led an elegant life of leisure in Newport each summer, Didion sees the palatial houses as monuments to the ethic of production: "The very houses are men's houses, factories, undermined by service railways, shot through with . . . vaults for table silver, equipment inventories of china and crystal . . . " Didion cannot imagine anyone relaxing in a house with a coal bin twice the size of the bedroom. Newport is for her a lesson engraved in stone, proof that "the production ethic led step by step to unhappiness, to restrictiveness, to entrapment in the mechanics of living." Just as she dramatized in *Run River* her belief that Americans in the West were trapped by the myth of the sacredness of their land, so in this essay she claims that Americans in the East fell victim to the myth that anything done on the grand scale is necessarily done well.

There is a profound tension in *Slouching Towards Bethlehem* between Didion's conviction that one must assume responsibility for one's own life and her fear that freedom of will is an illusion. The first section of "Los Angeles Notebook" pictures the city in the grip of the Santa Ana, a hot malevolent wind that sweeps through the city in the fall, increasing the crime and accident rates, and almost inevitably causing a devastating forest fire. "To live with the Santa Ana," Didion writes "is to accept, consciously or unconsciously, a deeply mechanistic view of human nature."

"Los Angeles Notebook" selects isolated events occurring in the city, events that reflect apprehension and hostility. One brief vignette features an all-night radio show on which the disc jockey moderates a dispute between a supporter of Helen Gurley Brown and a disapproving woman who wants to burn not only the book but its author. In another episode, an American at a party in Beverly Hills approaches the wife of an English actor and tries to make polite conversation about her husband:

> "I hear he's marvelous in this picture."
> She looks at the American for the first time. When she finally speaks she enunciates every word very clearly. "He . . . is . . . also . . . a . . . fag," she says pleasantly.

Although Didion places herself in only two of the episodes in "Los Angeles Notebook," we recall her assertion in the essay "On Keeping a Notebook" that "however dutifully we record what we see around us, the common denominator of all we see is always, transparently, shamelessly, the implacable 'I.'" The real subject of "Los Angeles Notebook" is Didion's own state of mind—insomniac, frightened, angry—a thoroughly desolate emotional landscape.

In the final episode of the notebook the anger has drained, leaving only a jaunty despair. Alone in a bar, Didion goes to a pay phone and calls a friend in New York. "'Where are you?', he says. 'In a piano bar in Enrico,' I say. 'Why?' he says. 'Why not,' I say." Her lines might have been spoken by Maria in *Play It As It Lays*, so vast is their emptiness. "Los Angeles Notebook" is a companion essay to "Slouching Towards Bethlehem." In the latter, Didion was the unobtrusive narrator, recording objectively what she saw and heard. In "Los Angeles Notebook" she is the main character who, like the children in Haight-Ashbury, cannot articulate any purpose to her actions. Both essays were written in 1967, a difficult year in her personal life, a turbulent year in the history of the country. Not until ten years later, when she wrote *The White Album*, was Didion able to sort out the causes of the emotional paralysis that gripped her in the late sixties—and when she did identify the causes, the Santa Ana wind was not among them.

Didion's choice of "Goodbye to All That" as the closing piece of the collection is a curious one for several reasons. The piece is a narrative account of the eight years

in which Didion lived in New York City, both the good
years in which she loved the city and her job at *Vogue* and
the bad years towards the end when, too depressed to
work, she found herself crying in improbable places like
Chinese laundries. At the end of the piece she and Dunne
return to the West Coast on a "leave of absence" which
turns out to be permanent. Los Angeles emerges as a
haven for Didion from those things in New York ("women
walking Yorkshire terriers, . . . Times Square in the
afternoon . . . ") which she could no longer tolerate; in
Los Angeles she could smell jasmine everywhere and see
the moon over the Pacific.

The problem is that the California we see in *Slouching
Towards Bethlehem* is not a pastoral refuge redolent of
jasmine and full moons, but a place of lost children and
devilish winds, of broken and bad dreams. In the pre-
ceding essay Los Angeles is presented as a place of tension
and hostility, where Didion goes alone to piano bars,
where freedom of will is an illusion blown away each fall
by winds that bring out the violence latent in us all.

Perhaps we are intended to see the ending of "Goodbye to All That" as ironic, or perhaps Didion put the piece
last to create a pun from its title. It seems more likely that
she did not wish to end the collection on the despairing
note of "Los Angeles Notebook," although the tense, brit-
tle fragments of that piece in fact sound the dominant
chord of the collection.

Nevertheless, the themes of "Goodbye to All That"
do fit with the central ideas of *Slouching*. The essay is a
dramatization of discontinuity, as Didion's excitement
about New York City is rather abruptly supplanted by
disillusion and depression. It also echoes her recurrent
stress on personal responsibility, for responsibility was the
painful lesson that she learned in New York. Her first
years there were like the experience of a child at a fair; she
had the feeling of being on holiday, of taking a vacation

from her "real life." Her depression began when she lost this illusion: "That was the year, my twenty-eighth, when I was discovering . . . that some things are in fact irrevocable and that it had counted after all, every evasion and every procrastination, every mistake, every word, all of it." The essay does belong in the collection but, as a piece about Didion in her twenties, it would have been more appropriate as the first or second essay in "Seven Places of the Mind," rather than the last.

Slouching Towards Bethlehem was not as thoroughly covered in the press as Didion's subsequent books, but it did receive a few intelligent reviews. Dan Wakefield in *The New York Times Book Review* praised not only the "grace, sophistication, nuance, irony" of Didion's prose, but also her willingness to enter into the lives of the persons about whom she is writing.[2] Wakefield is right; Didion succeeds as a reporter because she is open to the thoughts and feelings of others (certainly the brilliance of her piece on Haight-Ashbury results from the fact that she "stayed around a while, and made a few friends"). However, to meet people and situations without preconceived ideas about them is also to meet them without psychological defenses. Didion's capacity to intimately confront scenes of pain and confusion gives us a fresh vision of our own time and place, but as we will see in *The White Album*, this capacity exacted from her a high emotional toll.

6

The White Album

In 1968 the Beatles, the British foursome who swept the world of popular music in the sixties, released a double-record album of thirty songs in a blank white cover. Many of the songs are pointedly about the United States: "Back in the U.S.S.R." mocks the homey patriotism of the familiar phrase "good old U.S. of A."; "Rocky Racoon" is a saga of a shoot-out in a saloon in Dakota; "The Continuing Story of Bungalow Bill" is a parody of the legend of Buffalo Bill and a lament for American violence.

While a few of the lyrics are gentle love songs, in others the singer presents himself as suicidal, half-mad. In several songs the lyrics consist of a series of unrelated images; "Glass Onion," for example, contains images like "the cast iron shore" and "bent backed tulips" that are confused rather than clarified by their context. In songs like "Glass Onion" only the harmony of the music links the images together.[1]

Not only is there no unifying theme in the collection, but many of the lyrics contradict each other: "Revolution" rejects violence as a means of social change, but "Piggies" implies that rich capitalists deserve to be attacked physically. The popular name for this Beatles collection, "the white album," thus aptly reflects its nature. For white is the most paradoxical of colors—at once the lack of color and the presence of all colors, positive and reassuring in its association with light and purity, but also ambiguous or even sinister in its blank indefiniteness. The "terror of whiteness" has been especially prominent in American literature, finding its most powerful symbol in Herman Melville's white whale, Moby Dick.

Perhaps Didion was invoking this paradoxical quality of whiteness and its peculiarly American reverberations of ambiguity and horror when she took the name of the Beatles recording for the title piece of her collection of essays published in 1979. Her essay, like the Beatles album, consists of discontinuous fragments connected only by the voice that recounts them. The fifteen episodes of "The White Album" tell the story of the late sixties in the United States, a story in which Didion can perceive no purpose or coherence. The central metaphor of the essay, taken from filmmaking, recalls the random arrangement of images in the Beatles' lyrics: "I was meant to know the plot, but all I knew was what I saw: Flash pictures in variable sequence, images with no 'meaning' beyond their temporary arrangement, not a movie but a cutting room experience."

In the fifteen "flash cuts" of "The White Album" the public and the personal are sometimes alternated, sometimes fused. One of the first "flash cuts" is a psychiatric report written to define Didion's emotional state in the summer of 1968, when after an attack of vertigo and nausea she went to an outpatient psychiatric clinic in Santa Monica. The report concludes, "In her view she lives in a world of people moved by strange, conflicted, poorly comprehended, and, above all, devious motivations which commit them inevitably to conflict and failure."

In criticizing Didion's world, the psychiatrist assumes that in the real world motivation is fairly straightforward and behavior fairly rational. But the real world upon which Didion reports in the fourteen "flash cuts" following this report is peopled with the Ferguson brothers, who brutally murder an old man for no reason they can articulate; with a rock group called the Doors, whose lyrics "tended to suggest some range of the possible just beyond a suicide pact"; with Linda Kasabian, one of Charles Manson's "girls" who took part in the murders at the home of Sharon Tate and later turned state's evidence. After reading the fourteen fragments we conclude that perhaps Didion's world was indeed the "real" world in 1968, for these people do not act rationally and purposefully; they do not understand their own devious motivations and violent actions.

Nor did Didion understand her own motives during this period. She and her husband and daughter lived in a house emblematic of the time, a large rented house on Franklin Avenue in Los Angeles, a house with peeling paint, broken pipes and unrolled tennis courts in a "senseless-killing neighborhood" where all the houses were decaying because their owners were waiting for a change in the zoning laws so that they might tear down the houses and put up high-rise apartments. People seemed to come and go in this large barnlike house without coherent reason or pattern. Didion frequently encountered strangers in the entrance hall, people who gave specious reasons for being there. On one occasion she met a woman she had gone to school with in Sacramento who was now a private detective: "'They call us Dickless Tracys,' she said, idly but definitely fanning the day's mail on the hall table." Didion never knew whether the woman's visit was social or professional.

Like the house, the "self" that Didion presents in these fragments is emblematic of the time. She was a hostess not sure of the identity of her guests ("I knew where the sheets and towels were kept but I did not always know who was sleeping in every bed"); she was a reporter who, traveling without a watch, did not know the time; she was the patient of a neurologist who diagnosed the cause of her visual disturbances as multiple sclerosis, but then told her that this was "an exclusionary diagnosis, and meant nothing." The interviews that she conducted as a reporter (with Eldridge Cleaver, Linda Kasabian) and the events that she witnessed (the press conference of Huey Newton, the strike at San Francisco State College that took on the festive air of a holiday) seemed equally meaningless.

Even though Didion at times during this period experienced her life as "simple and sweet," with the smell of jasmine drifting through the open windows of the house on Franklin Avenue, it was shadowed by a sense of inevitable doom, "a demented and seductive vortical tension . . . building in the community." For Los Angeles, Didion believes, the tension broke on the day that Charles Manson and his followers murdered Sharon Tate Polanski and her friends on Cielo Drive, leaving as their calling card the title of a song from the Beatles' white album, "Helter Skelter," in which the speaker, coming down from a trip on drugs, links a sexual invitation to his girl friend with an expressed fear of destroying her. "Helter Skelter" means literally, of course, "in a disorderly fashion"; it was an appropriate comment, not only on the mass murder, but on the decade of the sixties in the United States.

With this event in August, 1969, "the paranoia was fulfilled," and the sixties came to a close. For Didion herself, however, the sixties did not end until the first month of 1971, when she moved with her husband and daughter to a "house on the sea" north of Los Angeles. Although they found relics of the sixties in the house, "after a while we did some construction, and between the power saws and the sea wind the place got exorcised."

"The White Album" is the story of the sixties, a story with a beginning and an end, but no plot, no moral, no rationally motivated characters. Although it is in some ways the same story that Didion told in *Slouching Towards Bethlehem*, here the perspective is different. In *Slouching* she was the woman sitting alone in a piano bar where an unemployed screen writer defined Santa Barbara with the single word "putresence," the woman in the midst of the nightmare. In "The White Album" Didion tells the story of the sixties from the perspective of a woman who has banished the demons of the nightmare through the written record of their devastation.

Most of the remaining pieces in *The White Album* do have a plot and a moral; the vast majority were written in the seventies, when Didion liked both herself and her life better, when she was able to see a pattern, although not always an ideal one, in both her own life and the lives of others. Minor changes that she made in some of the previously published essays are quite telling. The first part of "In the Islands," for example, originally appeared in *Life* in 1969; when she included this piece in *The White Album* Didion omitted its one truly cynical passage, a reference to a comment made to her by a man with whom she had once lived in New York. Crying as she packed her bag to leave him, she asked him how he could watch her:

He told me that a great many things had happened to him during the ten years before I knew him, and nothing much touched him anymore. I remember saying that I never wanted to get the way he was, and he looked at me a long while before he answered, "Nobody wants to," he said. "But you will."

I think about that quite a bit now.

Didion uses the incident in the original version of the piece to imply that her lover was right, that one reaches a point of not caring, of being proof against another's pain. Presumably Didion omitted this incident from the article as it appears in *The White Album* because she now believes that her lover was wrong—she, at least, can still be moved by suffering, whether her own or someone else's. Didion made other small editorial changes in several pieces in the collection, nearly all of them involving an updating of the "self," a freeing of the more optimistic voice that is the authentic Joan Didion of the seventies.

The voice has not lost its caustic irony when confronted with arrogance or its potent understatement when confronted with mediocrity, but it is generally a more mellow, accepting woman who speaks to us in the pages of *The White Album*. Didion is also less nostalgic in this collection; persons are less likely to be measured against an idealized version of frontier individualism, for she seems to realize and accept that the ethic of absolute self-reliance is not workable in a time when people must depend on each other. She still measures people by her strict values of personal responsibility and commitment, but a new value emerges in *The White Album*—cooperation in the interest of the community. These essays embody appreciation for the forms of teamwork that keep communities safe (the well-organized lifeguards on Zuma beach) and supply them with things essential for life (the men and women who operate the California State Water Project).

Like *Slouching Towards Bethlehem*, *The White Album* contains twenty essays, some purely reportorial and a few purely personal, most a mixture of the two modes. Space will not permit discussion of all twenty, but I will discuss the best, the worst (the only badly written essay that Didion ever published), and the most representative. It is significant that very many of the essays in *The White Album* take architectural structures as their subject (houses, churches, museums, dams, waterworks, and shopping centers), and in several other essays such structures, while not the true subject of the piece, figure prominently. These buildings represent man's shaping of formless materials into purposeful and relatively permanent structures; thus they are all symbols of order, although very few represent ideal patterns of order.

In the essays these structures are often symbolic of the men and women who live and work in them. The first essay to follow "The White Album," entitled "James Pike, American," opens with a description of Grace Episcopal Cathedral in San Francisco, "a curious and arrogantly secular monument" standing "directly upon the symbolic nexus of all old California money and power, Nob Hill."

The cathedral seems to embody perfectly the spirit of James Pike, erstwhile Bishop of California, who spent three million dollars to install images of Einstein, Thurgood Marshall and John Glenn in the clerestory windows, and in what struck Didion as a presumptuous act after generations of Episcopalians had given their pennies towards its completion, pronounced the cathedral "finished."

Didion traces the life of James Albert Pike from his poor childhood in Oklahoma to the "Solemn Requiem Mass" offered at his funeral in the cathedral he had "finished" in California. She sees him as a thoroughly secular figure, American in his unremitting ambition, contemporary in his readiness to shed people or ideas that become inconvenient and in his lack of sustained commitment to anything but himself. His widowed mother was determined to create an environment in which James would never be frustrated, and he expected the world to do the same. Raised a Catholic, James repudiated Catholicism at the age of eighteen, remaining an agnostic until, working in Washington after his graduation from Yale Law School, he discovered that "practically every churchgoer you meet in our level of society is Episcopalian." Soon afterwards James determined to become, not merely an Episcopalian, but Episcopal Bishop of California. When his first wife stood in his way, he "invented an ecclesiastical annulment to cover his divorce."

Didion sees Pike as a "great literary character" because of the vastness of both his arrogance and his imagination. Faced with any unpleasant fact, he invented a solution to make it palatable. When his son committed suicide, Pike claimed to have talked with him via seance: "If death was troubling then start over and reinvent it as 'The Other Side.' If faith was troubling, then leave the church and reinvent it as 'The Foundation for Religious Transition.'" Shortly after leaving the church, Pike drove into the Jordanian desert in a rented car with his new wife and two bottles of Coca-Cola. Although his young wife

escaped alive, he did not. Didion finds his hubris reflected
also in this final endeavor; his purpose was to experience
the wilderness as Christ had, but he apparently lacked
some of Christ's resources. The desert in which he died
serves as symbol of his spiritual aridity, just as the
cathedral represents his secular pride.

In the final essay in *The White Album*, "Quiet Days in
Malibu," Didion portrays a man who stands in sharp contrast to James Albert Pike. She met Amado Vasquez in a
greenhouse; having always felt a temperamental affinity
for greenhouses, Didion wandered one day into a greenhouse at Arthur Freed Orchids, a nursery near her house
in Malibu. Vasquez was head grower for Arthur Freed;
he was also, she discovered some time later, one of
perhaps two dozen truly great orchid breeders in the
world. Because he seemed willing to take "only the most
benign notice" of her presence there, she acquired the
habit of eating lunch in what seemed to her "the most
beautiful greenhouses in the world—the most aqueous
filtered light, the softest tropical air, the most silent cloud
of flowers."

So Didion came to know a good deal about orchids
and the tremendous skill and commitment required to
breed them. Vasquez pollinated them at full moon and
high tide: full moon because over their sixty-five million
years of evolution their period of fertility came to coincide
with the time when they would be visible to the night-
flying moth, and high tide because their moisture content
responds to the movements of the tide. Vasquez allowed
her to handle the plants and enjoyed showing her "some
marginal difference in the substance of the petal or the
shape of the blossom." After he fertilized a plant, it was
tended by his wife Maria "in a sterile box with sterile
gloves and sterile tools."

Not until the day that Didion talked to the owner of
the nursery did she realize that the stud plants she handled
were worth from ten thousand to seven hundred and fifty
thousand dollars; Vasquez talked of their beauty, but

never mentioned their dollar value. They occasionally talked of other things: Vasquez explained to her that he had never become a U.S. citizen because he could not shake from his mind an image he knew to be irrational: "standing before a judge and stamping on the flag of Mexico." Didion writes that she had never "talked to anyone so direct and unembarrassed about the things he loved." Vasquez loved his native country, his wife and children, and orchids.

In 1978 Vasquez bought from Arthur Freed his entire stock of orchids and was in the process of moving it to his own nursery down the canyon when a fire storm devastated the main greenhouse at Arthur Freed Orchids. When Didion next saw him he told her simply, "I lost three years." But he had no intention of giving up: "You want today to see flowers . . . we go down to the other place." The orchid, a plant associated with mysterious jungles, can live for well over a century without showing signs of age. In this essay it is for Didion a symbol of the rich depth of Vasquez' character and the tenacity of his commitments. The greenhouse in which they met has symbolic value, too; it represents the warm, quiet friendship that grew between them, a haven of order, peace, and beauty. When they returned after the fire to find the greenhouse "a range not of orchids but of shattered glass and melted metal and the imploded shards of the thousands of chemical beakers that had held the Freed seedlings," Didion writes, "for an instant I thought we would both cry."

Some of the architectural structures in *The White Album*, like the greenhouse in Malibu, are emblematic of the men and women who work in them; others reflect their builders and designers. "Many Mansions" is the Biblical title of an essay comparing the empty house built by the state of California to the specifications of Ronald and Nancy Reagan, the "new official residence for governors of California," with the old Victorian Gothic house at 16th and H Streets in Sacramento, the governor's residence from 1903 until the day that Ronald Reagan took office. As Didion walked through the new house located on the bank of the American River, she tried unsuccessfully to discover what the one million four hundred thousand dollars had purchased. Although the walls resemble local abode, they are in fact concrete blocks; although the exposed beams resemble native redwood, they are in fact construction-grade lumber stained brown. The only distinctive features she discovered in the house are the large number of exterior wood-and-glass doors (thirty-five) and the $90,000 worth of teak cabinetry (none of it bookcases, most of it for "refreshments").

Jerry Brown refused to live in the "house on the river"; although he never saw it, he called it a "Taj Mahal." Others termed it "a monument to the colossal ego" of Ronald Reagan. Didion concludes that it is neither of these; it is rather "an enlarged version of a very common kind of California tract house, a monument not to colossal ego but to a weird absence of ego, a case study in the architecture of limited possibilities, . . . flattened out, mediocre . . . and as devoid of privacy as the lobby area in a Ramada Inn." Although the house did not appeal to Jerry Brown, he had a political problem in articulating his distaste, for it is the type of house in which many of his constituents live.

Although she knew the old "Governor's Mansion" from girlhood visits there, Didion took the public tour with a group who failed to share her affection for the unique house of "three stories and a cupola and the face of Columbia the Gem of the Ocean worked into the molding over every door." While others on the tour lamented the stairs and the waste space in the wide hallways, Didion delighted in the large private bedrooms, the small sewing and ironing rooms. As the only woman in the group who knew that the purpose of the marble-top table in the kitchen was to roll out pastry, she realized that most women today cook by defrosting food in microwave ovens. This sign of changing values evokes in her a playful mood of self-mockery: "I felt very like the heroine of Mary McCarthy's *Birds of America*, the one who located America's moral decline in the disappearance of the first course."

In "On the Mall" Didion pokes fun at her own youthful ambition to be a builder of shopping centers. She acquired this ambition when, at the age of twenty-four, she realized that she wanted to spend her time writing fiction. She explains, "I had it in my head that a couple of good centers might support this habit less taxingly than a pale-blue office at Vogue." In pursuit of this aim she took a correspondence course in shopping-center theory that taught her the proper placement of the major tenant. In the essay, however, Didion also offers a serious analysis of the role played by the shopping center in American life. The shopping center movement began in the late forties and fifties, an adjunct to certain other phenomena of the time: the "baby boom," the consumer revolution, the growth of suburbia. Shopping centers remain a central feature of American life because they serve two major needs. They are, first, equalizers, "toy garden cities in which no one lives but everyone consumes," for they cater to both rich and poor. They are also sedatives, places where one can escape the self, for on the mall no one can make demands on you, reach you on the telephone, force you to confront an unpleasant problem.

More than "climate-controlled monuments" to the fifties, shopping centers are here to stay, testimony to a certain frailty in the American character, but hardly a sinister cultural development. Didion concludes the essay by confessing that she herself suspends all intelligent judgment on the mall; on one occasion in Honolulu she bought caramel corn, straw hats, nail polish, and a toaster at a center where she had gone to pick up *The New York Times*: "I do not wear hats, nor do I like caramel corn. I do not use nail enamel. Yet flying back over the Pacific I regretted only the toaster."

A structure that seems to Didion to exist in perfect harmony with its founder is the Getty Museum, a splendid re-creation of a Roman villa built high above the Pacific Coast in Malibu. Although Getty never saw the museum, he closely supervised its construction and acquisitions. Considered garish and vulgar in Establishment art circles, the museum nonetheless draws crowds so huge that one must call in advance for an appointment. Getty was not disappointed by the museum's poor press, since he built it not for the critics but for the public. To insure that admission would remain forever free of charge, he left the Getty the largest endowment of any museum in the world. Although Didion apparently wrote "The Getty" without direct personal knowledge of Getty, she seems to have read his character accurately from the structure itself. A quintessential democrat, Getty welcomed to his home in Surrey not only his art curators, but the museum's security guards and parking lot attendants. The Getty stands as a "palpable contract between the very rich and the people who distrust them least"—i.e., "the public."

A second theme of this essay ties it to *Slouching Towards Bethlehem* as well as to Didion's fiction. Art critics, she contends, are hopeless romantics who see the past as they wish it had been, a time of bleached and mellowed murals, faded bronze, and silent fountains. She sees in the Getty a lesson in realism: "ancient marbles were not always attractively faded and worn. Ancient marbles once appeared just as they appear here: as strident, opulent evidence of imperial power and acquisition." The obese, heavily ornamented furniture of the Getty may not be tasteful by the standards of contemporary critics, but it was the furniture that rich Europeans chose as tangible proof of their wealth. The Getty forces us to rethink our notions of classical and European art, to see them as forms of social as well as aesthetic expression.

"The Getty" reflects the attempt to realistically integrate past and present, an attempt that was Didion's chief

concern in *Slouching Towards Bethlehem*. What she discovered in the essays of that collection, however, was primarily discontinuity and disorder. Her vision of the
seventies in *The White Album* is very different; while not
overlooking either folly (the empty governor's residence in
Sacramento) or sorrow (the burial of a young man killed
in Vietnam in 1970), the vision is fundamentally orderly.
All of the man-made structures that figure centrally in
these essays are both real and psychological defenses
against a meaningless, disorderly universe. Museums are
a way of ordering the past; houses and dams impose order
on the present and the future, while churches encompass
all three of time's dimensions through the concepts of
religion.

In an irony of which she is delightfully aware, Didion
reserves her reverence in this collection for a thoroughly
secular structure, the Operations Control Center of the
California State Water Project. "Holy Water" is an
apotheosis of this technological miracle that serves mil-
lions of people who are scarcely aware of it. Located in
Sacramento, the California State Water Project brings
water from mountains and rivers across deserts "through
aqueducts and siphons and pumps and forebays and after-
bays and weirs and drains" to irrigate the arid regions of
the West Coast. Speaking in the specialized language of
her religion, Didion worships this powerful "God" that
proves man and nature need not be at odds. Like any true
believer, she is versed in the mysteries of the religion: she
knows that it takes two days to move a delivery of water
down through Oroville into the Delta and another six
days to bring this same water down from the Delta and
pump it from the floor of the San Joaquin Valley over the
Tehachapi Mountains. The planning and execution of
deliveries to each of the project's five divisions is enormously complex, even with "the best efforts of several human minds and that of a Univac 418." Didion sees the

functions of these minds as sacramental and desires for
herself the power of administering the sacraments: "I
wanted to be the one, that day, who was shining the
olives, filling the gardens, and flooding the daylong val-
leys like the Nile. I want it still."

Didion's discovery of the technological and social
structures that provide order is a major unifying theme of
The White Album. The opposite theme, social structures
that create chaos, is also present. In some essays this chaos
is merely annoying: in "Bureaucrats" Didion analyzes the
traffic jams and minor accidents resulting from experi-
mentation with diamond lanes on the Los Angeles free-
ways, as well as the jargon used to justify the experiment.
In other essays the disorder is terrifying: in the second
episode of "Notes Toward a Dreampolitik," Didion analyzes the values romanticized in "bike movies," a genre of
low-budget films aimed at adolescents in which the heroic
motorcycle gangs respond to small frustrations with rape
and murder before roaring off into the sunset. In these
pieces Didion effectively evaluates negative aspects of
American culture by clearly defining the problem and
sharply illustrating it.

One essay in the collection, however, represents a
disquieting exception to this description of Didion's ability
to assess American culture objectively. Entitled "The
Women's Movement," the piece appeared originally in
The New York Times Book Review of July 30, 1972, where it
generated fierce controversy. It is not properly a book review, however (although Didion listed fifteen books, she
refers to only three of them in the article and does not re-
produce the list in *The White Album*); it is rather a jumbled
attack on the women's movement, a one-sided mixture of
half-truth and wild generalization. As nearly as it is possible to sort them out, its main quarrels with the women's
movement seem to be four. Didion opens the article by
stating that although the movement had political potential
as a Marxist movement, it has become mired in the triv-

ial. This part of the argument is confused by her refusal to acknowledge that women constitute a "class" in the Marxist sense and by her studious avoidance of those authors (such as Kate Millet in *Sexual Politics*) who do perceive the issues as political. Also, because she does not distinguish the first women's movement, which began in the mid-nineteenth century, from the second, contemporary movement, it is impossible to know what she means by its political potential.

The article's subsequent arguments are somewhat clearer. Didion disapproves of feminist interpretations of literature, for fiction "has certain irreducible ambiguities," and, as a writer of fiction, she "remains committed mainly to the exploration of moral distinctions and ambiguities." This is an important statement of Didion's view of the novelist and is in fact borne out by her own novels, but she does not succeed in demonstrating that feminist criticism is inevitably reductive; in fact, she names no feminist critics.

Her third objection to the movement is that it has led women to deny their unique sexuality. Didion makes clear that she thinks of heterosexual intercourse as both natural and emotionally compelling; she thinks that women who deny this fact are avoiding "adult sexual life itself: how much cleaner to stay forever children." According to Didion, proponents of the movement also deny other dimensions of female sexuality: "the transient stab of dread and loss which accompanies menstruation," as well as the essential mystery of womanhood, "that dark involvement with blood and birth and death." One may take issue with this view of woman's sexuality, but it is at least coherent and also consistent with the experience of Didion's own fictional heroines.

Didion's final argument is that the movement has done women a disservice by encouraging them to perceive themselves as victims. She pities women who responded to movement rhetoric by throwing over their husbands and children and venturing forth to conquer the world, and she provides striking examples of naiveté: a mother who leaves her children to go to New York to "become this famous writer," a suburban housewife who wants "the chance to respond to the bright lights and civilization of the Big Apple."

Didion's examples are valid illustrations of women seeking, not adult fulfillment, but a dream of romance. She is not convincing, however, when she claims that any woman who is discriminated against or exploited has only herself to blame:

That many women are victims of condescension and exploitation and sex-role stereotyping was scarcely news, but neither was it news that other women are not: nobody forces women to buy the package.

This attitude is strikingly different from that found in the series of articles she wrote for *Mademoiselle* in the early sixties, articles that documented the many jobs in finance and government that were closed to women college graduates and showed, in fact, that in some cities virtually the only positions open to educated women were secretarial.

It is unfortunate that Didion did not rewrite this article, for it contains many ideas helpful to an understanding of her fiction. As it stands, however, it is anomalous in the collection for its lack of focus and precision, and especially for its uncontrolled use of sarcasm and overstatement. Abandoning her usual concrete dramatic method, Didion relies in this essay almost wholly on generalization, presenting only the excesses of the movement (and exaggerating those) and thus completely ignoring the complexity of the issues she is discussing.

"The Women's Movement" is followed by two essays on individual women artists, the English novelist Doris Lessing and the American painter Georgia O'Keeffe. Didion's distaste for Lessing's fiction tells us a good deal about her own view of the proper realm of fiction. Didion scorns the quest for ultimate solutions to social problems embodied in Lessing's fiction because she does not believe such solutions exist; as she wrote in a later essay in this collection, "On the Morning After the Sixties," "the heart of darkness lay not in some error of social organization but in man's own blood." Didion also objects to the quest because it has led to an explicit didacticism in Lessing's fiction. Fiction should be about people rather than ideas, Didion believes, and its moral must be implicit within the story of what happens to those people: "*Madame Bovary* told us more about bourgeois life than several generations of Marxists have, but there does not seem much doubt that Flaubert saw it as an artistic problem." The essay reveals Didion's own bias in favor of traditional realistic fiction into which the author never intrudes his own voice, his own opinions.

Didion's view of the role of the artist is further clarified by her admiring essay on Georgia O'Keeffe. Unlike Lessing, O'Keeffe never thought of herself as an intellectual, never wove abstract theories about art: she simply painted what she saw. Didion sees O'Keeffe as a prototype of a strong individualistic woman undefeated by the male-dominated art world:

"The men" believed it impossible to paint New York, so Georgia O'Keeffe painted New York. "The men" didn't think much of her bright color, so she made it brighter. The men yearned toward Europe so she went to Texas, and then New Mexico.

Although Didion does not note them, there are many parallels between her and O'Keeffe. They are both western Americans who took their country as subject. O'Keeffe in her painting, and Didion in her fiction (especially *A Book of Common Prayer*), each created sharp, bright, sometimes harsh, images. Perhaps most important, they each took their inspiration from a perceived reality rather than an abstract idea. One recalls Didion's statement that each of her three novels began from a visual, sensuous image imprinted on her mind and memory.

Didion tells the story of her seven-year-old daughter's response to one of O'Keeffe's huge paintings of clouds. After studying the canvas for some time and learning the name of the painter, Quintana told her mother, "I need to talk to her." Didion saw behind the little girl's remark a principle to which she subscribes absolutely:

She was assuming that the glory she saw in the work reflected a glory in its maker, that the painting was the painter as the poem is the poet, that every choice one made alone—every word chosen or rejected, every brush stroke laid or not laid down—betrayed one's character. *Style is character.*

Believing that style is character, Didion edits her own work rigorously, on occasion pondering at some length whether to place a comma after a particular phrase. The style of her essays is almost invariably acclaimed, although it has been less carefully scrutinized than the quality of her thought. It is a highly artful style, combining many traditional rhetorical techniques with some less traditional ones, and governed overall by an acute sensitivity to cadence, the rising and falling rhythms of words. The examples of Didion's style that follow are taken from various essays in *Slouching Towards Bethlehem* and *The White Album*.

One of Didion's favorite rhetorical devices is parallelism, the casting of like ideas in like grammatical form. She uses parallelism to organize whole passages (the passage above defining O'Keeffe's relationship to the "men" of the art world is a good example) and to organize the ideas in a single sentence: "I could write a syndicated column for teenagers under the name "Debbi Lynn" or I could smuggle gold into India or I could become a $100 call girl, and none of it would matter."[2] In this example Didion throws emphasis on the final clause by breaking the parallel structure.

One finds examples of parallelism, a most traditional

rhetorical device, in nearly all of Didion's essays. She is also fond of antithesis, in which *opposed* ideas are arranged in parallel form:

To have that sense of one's intrinsic worth which constitutes self-respect is potentially to have everything: the ability to discriminate, to love and to remain indifferent. To lack it is to be locked within oneself, paradoxically incapable of either love or indifference.[3]

Didion controls the pace of her prose by a careful balancing of long and short sentences. In the following passage she places a short simple sentence after a long paratactic (loosely coordinated) one:

When I first saw New York I was twenty, and it was summertime, and I got off a DC-7 at the old Idlewild temporary terminal in a new dress which had seemed very smart in Sacramento but seemed less smart already, even in the old Idlewild temporary terminal, and the warm air smelled of mildew and some instinct, programmed by all the movies I had ever seen and all the songs I had ever heard sung and all the stories I had ever read about New York, informed me that it would never be quite the same again. In fact it never was.[4]

The long sentence leaves the reader quite as breathless as the young woman it describes, and the short sentence acquires sharp emphasis through its brevity.

When Didion wants to establish intimacy with the reader, she addresses him directly: "You see the point. I want to tell you the truth, and already I have told you about the wide rivers."[5] The impression of sincerity created by the confessional form of these sentences is supported by the simple diction; of the twenty-one words in the two sentences, eighteen are monosyllables. These monosyllabic sentences illustrate Didion's use of sound in support of meaning.

A figure of sound to which Didion is very partial is alliteration (repetition of initial consonants): "To think of 'living' there was to reduce the miraculous to the mundane"[6]; "The princess is caged in the consulate"[7]; "the hot dry Santa Ana wind that comes down through the passes at 100 miles an hour and whines through the eucalyptus windbreaks and works on the nerves."[8] In the first example the alliteration highlights the contrast of "miraculous" and "mundane." In the second it calls attention to a certain incongruity: "princesses" and "cages" are found in fairy tales, but "consulates" are real and contemporary. In the final example alliteration emphasizes (perhaps even imitates) the unpleasant sound of the wind.

A figure of thought common to Didion's fiction and her essays is incongruity, the yoking of unlike ideas. The incongruity is especially striking when the unlike ideas are cast in parallel grammatical form: "This is the California where it is possible to live and die without ever eating an artichoke, without ever meeting a Catholic or a Jew."[9] The unlike ideas linked in this sentence are, of course, "eating an artichoke" and "meeting a Catholic or a Jew." A dramatic use of incongruity is found in the thesis sentence of Didion's essay on Michael Laski:

I know something about dread myself, and appreciate the elaborate systems with which some people manage to fill the void, appreciate all the opiates of the people, whether they are as accessible as alcohol and heroin and promiscuity or as hard to come by as faith in God or History.

The sentence startles by its linking of "alcohol and heroin and promiscuity" with "faith in God or History." The sentence also illustrates another characteristic of Didion's style, the use of a familiar image ("opiates of the people") in a context that expands its meaning. "Opiate of the people" was originally a metaphor for religion; Didion uses the phrase to refer to habits usually considered "bad" as well as to describe modes of faith.

Didion's prose is rich with concrete images. Sometimes these images are literal representations:

We watched the coffin being carried to the grave and we watched
the pallbearers lift the flag, trying to hold it taut in the warm
trade wind. The wind was blowing hard, toppling the vases of
gladioli set by the grave . . .[10]

Some of her images are metaphors, often strikingly contemporary ones:

To do without self-respect, . . . is to be an unwilling audience of
one to an interminable documentary that details one's failings,
both real and imagined, with fresh footage spliced in for every
screening.[11]

In her personal essays, especially, Didion is fond of allusions to figures from history and literature: "To say that
Waterloo was won on the playing fields of Eton is not to
say that Napoleon might have been saved by a crash program in cricket."[12]

To generalize about Didion's style is difficult because
it is so various in its use of rhetorical and stylistic devices.
It ranges widely in diction, using both simple and esoteric
words; in sentence structure, using long and short
sentences, loosely and tightly coordinated ones; in tone,
from mocking irony to straightforward praise or blame; in
manner, from the most intimate to the rather formal.
Two generalizations can safely be made, however: first,
Didion's style is invariably graceful, for she has a practiced ear for the rhythms of language; second, her style is
never inflated—every word counts.

Didion developed the concision and sharpness of
style for which she is known during her years at *Vogue*
after graduating from Berkeley. She did not have it in
1960, when she did a series of articles for *Mademoiselle*
on the lives of young women in various American cities.
The articles are informative and successful at capturing
the uniqueness of each city, but in style they incline to
redundancy:

Why do the girls go? Whatever their conscious reasons, most
go with the half-remembered sense, rooted deep in all our

folklore, that to go West is to open a frontier—perhaps spiritual if no longer geographical. . . . Some go under the pervasive delusion that the Western cities are still wide open—offering the same social and economic mobility that the West did seventy-five years ago. Some go for a career, some for a husband, and some for the climate. Those who go for the climate emerge the happiest.[13]

By 1961 Didion was beginning to hone her skills as a stylist. "On Self-Respect," an essay famous for its polished use of allusion and antithesis, was written in that year; yet in the same year she published a piece in *Vogue* on a similar topic that is flat and occasionally preachy. In each of the following two examples she uses allusion to suggest the concept of individual integrity; one has tremendous vitality, while the other rests upon clichés:

We flatter ourselves by thinking this compulsion to please others an attractive trait: a gist for imaginative empathy, evidence of our willingness to give. *Of course* I will play Francesca to your Paolo, Helen Keller to anyone's Annie Sullivan: no expectation is too misplaced, no role too ludicrous.[14]

There is no charm strong enough, no sedative potent enough, to enable us to be all things to all people: to try to be Hetty Green at four o'clock, Guinevere at five, and Caroline English at six is finally to forget whoever it is we see in the mirror.[15]

Not until 1964 did Didion's writing invariably display the poise and freshness found in her two collections. In that year she did a book review of Whalen's *The Founding Father: The Story of Joseph P. Kennedy* that one hopes she will someday convert into an essay on Kennedy, for its insight into the American character matches anything found in her pieces on John Wayne and Howard Hughes.[16] Throughout 1964 and 1965 she wrote innumerable movie reviews for *Vogue*, all of remarkable polish and wit. Her persistent animosity to films that seek overtly to convey a truth (*The Victors*; *Judgment at Nuremburg*) is her greatest weakness as a film critic, although it is

entirely consistent with both her theory and her practice
in the novel. Her reviews show a special sensitivity to
films that portray women's experience (so long as that experience is part of a story, and not didactically presented).
Against those critics who scorned *The Pumpkin Eater* as
"merely personal," Didion praises both the role and the
performance of Anne Bancroft as Mrs. Armitage:

In Harrods, sealed off by her own despair from all the shoppers
and clerks and piano tuners, alone among the faceless manne-
quins . . . she begins, abruptly, to cry. I have never before seen
so accurate an approximation of what "depression" means.[17]

Between *Slouching* and *The White Album*, Didion has
collected all of the columns she wrote for *Life* and *The
Saturday Evening Post* in 1967, 1968 and 1969, with two
very fine exceptions. "On the Last Frontier with VX and
GB" explores the attitudes of residents of Hermiston,
Oregon, toward the vast concrete mounds of nerve gas
stored just outside the town at Umatilla Army Depot.
Most residents were bothered neither by the threat of
death (almost certain if leakage should occur) nor the
ugliness of the "ominously regular mounds, reinforced
concrete covered with sod and sagebrush, 1,001 mounds
rising from the earth in staggered rows,"[18] for the depot
spelled growth and prosperity to them. The article was too
late for *Slouching* (where it would have fit nicely as an
eighth "Place of the Mind") and inappropriate for *The
White Album*, whose unifying image is one of architectural
structures that represent positive qualities such as faith
and stability.

For the December 19 issue of *Life* in 1969 Didion
wrote a profoundly personal piece that also has a seasonal
truth for all. "In Praise of Unhung Wreaths and Love" is
her description of the guilt she felt at being separated from
her small daughter the week before Christmas. She is in
New York with her husband working on a script, wishing
that she were home making pomegranate jelly or singing

carols with her daughter, when she realizes that her feeling is essentially false:

Watching an AP wire in an empty office is precisely what I want to be doing: women do not end up in empty offices by accident, any more than three-year-olds and their mothers need to make pomegranate jelly together to learn about family love. I am crying because I am tired and feeling sorry for myself and because the abstract that is Christmas seems always to heighten the capacity not only for self-pity but also for self-delusion, seems ever to make me forget that we design our lives as best we can. . . . Now I am going to wash my face and finish the work I like to do.

The article shows dramatically how the holiday season generates our hopeless attempts to meet sentimental ideals of "good cheer" and "family togetherness." It has a feminist theme, too, in her realization that "the baby will not be bereft on Christmas, nor will she ever know whether I strung her beads myself on the first of December or bought them on the twenty-fourth." One hopes that Didion will republish the piece in some future collection.

Three novels, two collections of essays, thirty uncollected essays, four short stories—these represent the sum of Didion's considerable achievement to date. One of the striking facts about this achievement is the evenness with which it is divided between fiction and nonfiction; the three novels quite precisely balance the seventy essays. In the brief conclusion which follows this chapter I will look at Didion's fiction and nonfiction writings together, identifying broadly their likenesses and their differences.

7

Conclusion

Few contemporary American writers are "American" in all the ways that Joan Didion is. Although she has visited Europe often, she has never written an essay on Europe, nor do we find a single European character in her fiction. Not only are all of her major fictional characters born and raised in the United States; they also bear no marks of European nationality, carry no memory traces of European traditions. Maria Wyeth has the same last name as a famous American painter; Edith Knight maintains her identity on a visit to Europe by keeping her watch on Pacific Standard Time. Although much of the action of *A Book of Common Prayer* takes place in Central America, its foreign setting serves only to throw Charlotte's character as *la norteamericana* into bolder relief.

In both her fiction and her essays, Didion sees the American character as often arrogant, often nostalgic, but invariably and quintessentially romantic, and thus deluded. Her more nostalgic characters are ever looking backward to the simplicity of childhood, finding there the source of the myth they are currently living: Maria Wyeth learned from her father that material success is life's easy and natural goal; Lily McClellan learned from her parents that no harm could come to her or her family in the Sacramento Valley. Her other characters have woven different myths: Charlotte Douglas, that all change is progress, that history moves people inevitably toward the

greater good; Grace Strasser-Mendana, that every problem is susceptible of scientific solution. These illusions are
characteristically (although not exclusively) American,
and Didion also sees as characteristically American the
tenacity with which they are held and the naiveté with
which they are expressed.

Against these romantic myths Didion portrays the
reality of the emptiness of material success, the disintegration of the family, and social and economic revolution
that do not, in any moral sense at least, constitute progress. Her characters must either recognize this reality (a
recognition that may produce madness, as it does in the
case of Maria Wyeth) or be destroyed by it, as Lucille
Miller and Charlotte Douglas are. Among Didion's heroines only Lily McClellan and Grace Strasser-Mendana
have the resilience to confront the realities of chaos and
evil and still find something in life worth affirming.

Seeing herself as "American" as anyone, Didion is
constantly testing her own illusions against reality. In
some cases (the fantasy that Hawaii is a paradise), reality
gradually chips her illusions away; in others (the illusion
in the late sixties that she lived in a rational world) reality
assaults them so brutally that she approaches the thresh-
old of madness, perhaps averting it only by imposing the
form and order of language on her chaotic feelings. Although brought up with the same illusions as many of the
people she writes about, Didion, unlike most of them, is
ultimately an antiromantic realist.

Didion's writings are American in their characters,
in the myths by which these characters try to live their
lives, and in their tension between a vision of nature and
God as benevolent and a conflicting vision of nature and
the supernatural as fraught with danger and evil. Didion
sees in Americans the dissonance produced by a naive
confidence that they have a covenant with God coexisting
with a fear of omnipresent evil and imminent doom;
stemming from our Puritan heritage, this dissonance is
familiar to readers of nineteenth-century American

literature, for it is a dominant note in the fiction of Hawthorne and Melville.

Didion sharply dramatizes this tension in her essay "On Morality." Writing the essay in a motel in Death Valley, Didion describes her conviction that there are rattlesnakes outside and refers to the "sinister hysteria" of the desert air in "this country so ominous and terrible that to live in it is to live with antimatter." Yet across the road from her motel a group of old people who live in trailers in the valley have gathered at the Faith Community Church for a prayer sing. Irritable from the heat and the voice of coyotes on the desert, Didion is glad that she cannot hear the singers: "if I were also to hear those dying voices, those Midwestern voices . . . *rock of ages cleft for me*, I think I would lose my own reason." This same tension between a mysterious and often evil universe and a naive faith that God will make everything turn out "all right" pervades *A Book of Common Prayer*, as Charlotte Douglas optimistically pursues her charitable works in a city whose leader seeks to kill his brother, where "the bite of one fly deposits an egg which in its pupal stage causes human flesh to suppurate." In one form or another, this tension is found in all three of Didion's novels.

Nature is sometimes beautiful in Didion's writings ("green hops in leaf, blackbirds flying up from the brush in the dry twilight air"), but it is always latent with terror as well, for it can subdue man, reducing him to insignificance. Like the Mississippi River in Mark Twain's *Huck Finn*, the Sacramento River in *Run River* represents not only time, but also the power and mystery of nature to which man is subject. The forces of nature in Didion's writings—the Santa Ana winds, a forest fire burning out of control—often have the majestic, destructive power that Melville attributed to the great white whale. As Ishmael wonders whether the destruction of the *Pequod* reflects upon the evil of Moby Dick or the evil living in the sailors' hearts, so does Didion stress the same mystery. In the opening statement of *Play It As It Lays*, Maria asks, "What makes Iago evil?" and a few lines later, "Why should a coral snake need two glands of neurotoxic poison to survive while a king snake, *so similarly marked*, needs none." Like the heroes of Hawthorne and Melville, Didion's heroines inhabit a world in which good and evil are not merely social or political, but part of the impenetrable universe itself.

Whereas Didion certainly sees the subjects of her fiction and essays as American, she would probably be surprised to hear her work described as "woman's literature," especially since she has publically rejected the tenets of the women's movement. Yet all three of her novels are dominated by a woman's point of view, and all three portray in detail women's feelings about experiences that are exclusively feminine: childbirth, motherhood, abortion, menstruation, sexual submission to male demands. The relationship between mother and daughter is important in all three, and overshadows all other bonds in *Play It As It Lays*. Maria mourns her mother's death almost without intermission in the novel; on the morning of the abortion she wakes up crying for her, for "sometime in the night she had moved into a realm of miseries peculiar to women." Maria's feelings for her mother and her brain-damaged daughter are the only instances of genuine love in the novel; one cause of her madness is the fact that neither of them is available to her. In *A Book of Common Prayer* Charlotte's daughter is the mainstay of her life, and thus her life falls apart when Marin leaves. At the end of the novel we learn that her memories of closeness to Marin were not essentially false; when Grace prods Marin by asking about her trip with her mother to the Tivoli Gardens, she touches a nerve that releases Marin's grief for her mother's death. All of Didion's heroines are mothers, and all are deeply involved with their children.

Although men in Didion's fiction often lack the power to express love or other emotion, they have a power to act, to change the real world, that women do not. In *Play It As It Lays* men are sometimes perceived as sexual objects, but women are so invariably seen in this way that Larry Kulik believes he is complimenting Maria when he tells her husband, "What I like about your wife, Carter, is she's not a cunt." In *Run River* the chivalrous attitude of the men would never permit a comment like Kulick's, yet that same attitude prevents women from engaging in meaningful work. To Everett's expression of dismay at the condition into which the ranch has fallen during his absence, Martha quite aptly retorts that she could hardly be expected to run the ranch, when "I can't even write a check around here." With no activities permitted them except child-rearing and social entertaining, it is little wonder that Martha and Lily feel helpless. Lily explains to her husband why she won't gamble when they are in Nevada: "Women don't ever win, Everett, . . . because winners have to believe they can affect the dice."

Didion's women are fully realized characters; we may or may not like them, but we understand why they behave as they do. Her male characters are often shadowy by comparison; the reasons for their actions are often far from clear. Everett McClellan is convincing in many parts of *Run River*, but we never understand why, given his eagerness to settle down and become a rancher, he enlists in the army, leaving Lily alone with two babies and a querulous old man. Leonard Douglas is superb as a witty, harassed lawyer, but his behavior at crucial points in *A Book of Common Prayer* is also puzzling. He clearly cares enough about Charlotte to keep track of her, to go to New Orleans when their baby is born; why on earth does he allow her to drift about Central America with a dying baby? On one level the answer to these questions is obvious: Didion wished to manipulate the plots of the novels to isolate her heroines. But she could have given her male characters more plausible motives for their behavior, especially in the case of Everett, whose point of view dominates whole sections of the novel.

Didion's fictional women engage her immense talents as a realistic novelist; she draws each of them with fine, sharp brush strokes that reveal every dimension of their personalities, every connection between character and action. Although her men cannot be called flat characters, they do not fully compel the reader's credence, for their behavior is often inconsistent with their character as Didion has presented it.

A few feminist critics rejected Didion's first two novels because Lily and Maria are passive, traditional women who yearn for the stability and emotional closeness of the family, submit to men sexually, and, with the exception of their mothers, are uncomfortable with other adult women.[1] However, feminist criticism today is less likely to dictate to writers the kinds of characters they should create. In "Women's Literature," Elizabeth Janeway sensibly suggests that women's literature is not confined to that written by avowed feminists, but rather includes all literature that presents "women's experience from within," describing and evaluating it "in terms which can be various and individual but which are inherently the product of women's lives."[2] Didion's fiction fits this definition, and Janeway in fact cites *Play It As It Lays* as an instance of contemporary women's literature.

While Didion's experience as a woman has been transformed and expressed through her fictional characters, her essays, with few exceptions, are not written from a woman's perspective. The voice in the essays is that of an American, a Californian, a writer, even a "migraine personality," but seldom a woman writing of explicitly feminine experience. There are a few exceptions: "John Wayne: A Love Song" could not have been written by a man, and one of the themes of "On Going Home" is the double mother-daughter relationship. Yet nowhere in the essays do we find what appears everywhere in the fiction, what Didion has called "the irreconcilable difference" of being a woman: "that sense of living one's deepest life underwater, that dark involvement with blood and birth

and death." Female experience as Didion conceives of it is
not only personal and sexual, but also uncontrolled. In
her fiction she can distance herself from and exercise control over this experience in a way that would be impossible
to achieve in her autobiographical essays.

Although not written from the particular perspective
of a woman, Didion's essays appeal to most feminists for
several reasons. They assume that a woman is just as involved in the larger society as a man and that her ability to
observe and analyze that society is as keen as his. Many of
them belong to the journalist's tradition of aggressive,
even intrusive reporting. They embody many qualities
traditionally considered "masculine": bluntness, precision, objectivity, and a complete absence of sentimental-
ity. One must be glad that Didion does not restrict herself
to feminine experience in her essays; although many
women are currently writing about every aspect of
women's experience, there are few writers—male or
female—with her dramatic ability to present and evaluate
American culture.

In both her essays and her fiction Didion seeks to
render the moral complexity of contemporary American
experience, especially the dilemmas and ambiguities
resulting from the erosion of traditional values by a new
social and political reality. To this end, she violates the
conventions of traditional journalism whenever it suits
her purpose, fusing the public and the personal, frequently placing herself in an otherwise objective essay,
giving us her private and often anguished experience as a
metaphor for the writer, for her generation, and sometimes for her entire society.

In her fiction, on the other hand, Didion has found
that a traditional form and structure better suit her purpose. Unlike many other contemporary novelists, she
creates real settings, characters that behave with some
consistency, plots that have a beginning, middle, and
end. In her few pieces of literary criticism Didion defends
these traditions against the "new fiction" of Kurt

Vonnegut, Joseph Heller, and Bruce Jay Friedman. Lacking plot, structure, or consistent point of view, the new fiction, Didion feels, allows the author to abnegate his responsibility to make a moral statement:

To throw a picaresque character into a series of improvised situations is to stay as clear of a consistent point of view as one possibly can; all the old structural conventions automatically confer upon the novelist, whether he wants it or not, a point of view, a stance, a statement.[3]

In several different pieces she cites *Madame Bovary* as a model to be emulated: realistic in its smallest detail, traditional in structure and plot, it is a model that Didion aspires to, for it is the kind of novel that she believes comes closest to the truth. When she speaks of the truth, Didion thinks not of a political or religious truth—of any ideology—but of a setting forth of moral ambiguity, an ordering of life's moral complexity. To this end, style and artifice are not the enemies of truth, but the means to approach it:

Everyone wants to tell the truth, and everyone recognizes that to juxtapose even two sentences is necessarily to tell a lie, to tell less than one knows, to distort the situation. . . . To write with style is to fight lying all the way. Nonetheless, this is what must be done or we . . . tell nothing.[4]

Implicit in Didion's view of the writer's responsibility is her conviction that, however multiple and ambiguous it may be, truth exists and can be approached by the writer with the courage and skill to project a coherent, realistic vision. Her own vision reveals to us the moral condition of contemporary Americans, living by illusions as fragile as fine china, clinging to shards of broken dreams, yet often redeemed by an immense potential for love and commitment. Thus, while preternaturally attuned to every false note in American culture, Didion yet holds out to us the possibility of integrity, integrity based on rigorous and continual self-scrutiny. "Style is character," she has said. The care that she devotes to every paragraph, the years spent on a single novel, the endless revisions, the novels and essays begun and laid aside—all attest to her struggle for integrity. We accept her criticism of us because it stems from the same drive, "to fight lying all the way." For Didion, integrity of style and integrity of character are one.

Notes

1. JOAN DIDION: A BIOGRAPHICAL ESSAY

1. Michiko Kakutani, "Joan Didion: Staking Out California," *The New York Times Magazine*, 10 June 1979, p. 38.
2. Joan Didion, "Notes from a Native Daughter," in *Slouching Towards Bethlehem* (New York: Farrar, Straus & Giroux, 1968), p. 172.
3. Didion, "Notes," p. 173.
4. Ibid.
5. Kakutani, "Staking", p. 40.
6. Didion, "On Keeping a Notebook," in *Slouching*, p. 133.
7. Kakutani, "Staking," p. 36.
8. Didion, "Notes," p. 174.
9. Didion, "Notes," p. 181.
10. Didion, "Notes," p. 174.
11. Didion, "Letter from Paradise," in *Slouching*, p. 189.
12. Didion, "In Bed," in *The White Album* (New York: Simon and Schuster, 1979), p. 169.
13. Kakutani, "Staking," p. 40.
14. Sara Davidson, "A Visit With Joan Didion," *New York Times Book Review*, 3 April 1977, p. 38.
15. Didion, "Notebook," p. 140.
16. Didion, "Many Mansions," in *White Album*, p. 71.
17. Didion, "On The Morning After The Sixties," in *White Album*, p. 207.
18. Didion, "Why I Write," *New York Times*, 5 December 1976, p. 2.
19. Ibid.
20. Didion, "Morning After," pp. 206–207.
21. Didion, "On Self-Respect," in *Slouching*, p. 143.

22. Didion, "Goodbye to All That," in *Slouching*, p. 226.
23. Didion, "Goodbye," pp. 228–230.
24. Didion, "Goodbye," p. 234.
25. Kakutani, "Staking," p. 44.
26. Didion, "A Problem of Making Connections," *Life*, 5 December 1969, p. 34.
27. Didion, "Goodbye," p. 237.
28. Didion, "Goodbye," p. 226.
29. Alfred Kazin, "Joan Didion: Portrait of a Professional," *Harper's*, 243: December 1971, p. 114.
30. Didion, "Making Connections," p. 34.
31. Didion, "Letter from Paradise, 21° 19′ N., 157° 52′ W.," in *Slouching*, p. 187.
32. Didion, "The White Album," in *White Album*, p. 12.
33. Didion, "White Album," p. 14.
34. Didion, "White Album," pp. 12–13.
35. Didion, "In The Islands," in *White Album*, p. 135.
36. Didion, "White Album," p. 16.
37. "Writers Roost." *Vogue*, 1 October 1972, 146–148.
38. Davidson, "A Visit", p. 38.
39. Susan Braudy, "A Day in the Life of Joan Didion," *Ms*. 5: February 1977, p. 108.
40. Kakutani, "Staking," p. 50.
41. Didion, "Quiet Days in Malibu," *White Album*, p. 223.
42. Didion, "White Album," pp. 14–15.
43. Ibid.
44. Kakutani, "Staking," p. 50.
45. Davidson, "A Visit," p. 38.
46. Ibid.
47. Didion, "The Women's Movement," *White Album*, pp. 112–113.
48. Didion, "Why I Write," p. 2.
49. Ibid.
50. Braudy, "A Day," pp. 107–108.

2. *Play It As It Lays*

1. Catherine Barnes Stevenson, "Film as Metaphor in Didion's *Play It As It Lays*," (Paper delivered at the Annual Spring Convention of the Northeast Modern Language

Association, North Dartmouth, Mass., 21 March, 1980), p. 2.

2. Joan Didion, "The Women's Movement," in *The White Album*, p. 117.

3. Vincent Canby, "Film Review," *New York Times*, 30 October 1972, 36:2.

4. Ibid.

5. John Leonard, "The Cities of the Desert, the Desert of the Mind," *New York Times*, 21 July 1970, p. 33.

6. Guy Davenport, "On the Edge of Being," *National Review*, 25 August 1970, p. 903.

3. *Run River*

1. D. H. Lawrence, "The Spirit of Place," *Studies in Classic American Literature* (New York, The Viking Press, 1964), p. 3.

2. Lawrence, "The Spirit of Place," pp. 6–7.

3. Joan Didion, "I Want to Go Ahead and Do It," review of *The Executioner's Song* by Norman Mailer, *New York Times Book Review*, 7 October 1979, p. 26.

4. Guy Davenport, "Midas' Grandchildren," *National Review*, May 1963, p. 371.

5. Didion, "Notes From A Native Daughter," in *Slouching Towards Bethlehem*, p. 173.

6. Sara Davidson, "A Visit With Joan Didion," *New York Times Book Review*, 3 April 1977, p. 38.

7. Miriam Ylvisaker, review of *Run River* in *Library Journal*, 1 June 1963, p. 2274.

8. *New Yorker*, 11 May 1963, p. 178.

4. *A Book of Common Prayer*

1. Sara Davidson, "A Visit with Joan Didion," *New York Times Book Review*, 3 April 1977, p. 8.

2. Peter S. Prescott, "Didion's Grace," *Newsweek*, 21 March 1977, p. 30.

3. Joyce Carol Oates, "A Taut Novel of Disorder," *New York Times Book Review*, 3 April 1977, p. 1.
4. Benjamin Stein, "Dinner in the Rain Forest," *National Review*, 10 June 1977, p. 678.
5. Susan Lardner, "Facing Facts," *New Yorker*, 20 June 1977, p. 117.
6. Frederic Raphael, "Grace Under Pressure," *Saturday Review*, 5 March 1977, p. 23.

5. *Slouching Towards Bethlehem*

1. Montaigne, M. E. *Principaux Chapitres et Extraits des "Essais"* (Paris: Librairie Hachette, 1934), p. 2.
2. Dan Wakefield, review of *Slouching Towards Bethlehem*, *New York Times Book Review*, 21 July 1968, p. 8.

6. *The White Album*

1. Lyrics from this album are copyright 1968 by Northern Songs Ltd, England.
2. Joan Didion, "Goodbye to All That," in *Slouching Towards Bethlehem*, p. 229.
3. Didion, "On Self-Respect," in *Slouching*, p. 147.
4. Didion, "Goodbye to All That," in *Slouching*, pp. 225–226.
5. Didion, "Notes from A Native Daughter," in *Slouching*, p. 178.
6. Didion, "Goodbye to All That," in *Slouching*, p. 231.
7. Didion, "The White Album," in *The White Album*, p. 11.
8. Didion, "Some Dreamers of the Golden Dream," in *Slouching*, p. 3.
9. Didion, "Some Dreamers," p. 4.
10. Didion, "In The Islands," *The White Album*, pp. 142–143.
11. Didion, "On Self-Respect," in *Slouching*, pp. 143–144.
12. Didion, "On Self-Respect," p. 147.
13. Didion, "San Francisco Job Hunt," *Mademoiselle*, September 1960, p. 128.
14. Didion, "On Self-Respect," in *Slouching*, pp. 147–148.
15. Didion, "Take No For An Answer," *Vogue*, 1 October 1961, p. 133.

16. Didion, "The World Was His Oyster," review of *The Founding Father: The Story of Joseph P. Kennedy*, *National Review*, 16: 1 December 1964, pp. 1604–1605.

17. Didion, "Vogue's Notebook: Movies," review of *The Pumpkin Eater*, *Vogue*, 1 January 1965, p. 66.

18. Didion, "On The Last Frontier With VX and GB," *Life*, 13 March 1970, p. 22.

7.   CONCLUSION

1. Catherine Stimpson, "The Case of Miss Joan Didion," *Ms.*, January 1973, pp. 36–41.

2. Elizabeth Janeway, "Women's Literature," in *Harvard Guide to Contemporary American Writing*, edited by Daniel Hoffman (Cambridge: Harvard University Press, 1979), p. 345.

3. Didion, "Questions About the New Fiction," *National Review*, 30 November 1965, p. 1101.

4 Ibid.

Bibliography

WORKS BY JOAN DIDION

Books

Run River. New York: Obolensky, 1963.

Slouching Towards Bethlehem. New York: Farrar, Straus & Giroux, 1968.

Play It As It Lays. New York: Farrar, Straus & Giroux, 1970.

A Book of Common Prayer. New York: Simon & Schuster, 1977.

Telling Stories. Berkeley, California: Bancroft Library, 1978.

White Album. New York: Simon & Schuster, 1979.

Articles

"Berkeley's Giant: The University of California." *Mademoiselle*, January 1960, pp. 88–91.

"San Francisco Job Hunt." *Mademoiselle*, September 1960, pp. 128–129.

"New York: the Great Reprieve." *Mademoiselle*, February 1961, p. 102.

"Jealousy: Is it a Curable Illness?" *Vogue*, June 1961, pp. 96–97.

"Take No for an Answer." *Vogue*, 1 October 1961, pp. 132–133.

"When It was Magic Time in Jersey." *Vogue*, 15 September 1962, pp. 33–35.

"Emotional Blackmail: An Affair of Every Heart." *Vogue*, 15 November 1962, pp. 116–117.

"Washington, D.C.: Anything Can Happen Here." *Mademoiselle*, November 1962, pp. 132–135.

"I'll Take Romance." *National Review*, 24 September 1963, pp. 246–249.

"Silver—To Have and to Hurl." *Vogue*, 1 April 1964, p. 60.

"Coming Home." *Saturday Evening Post*, 11 July 1964, p. 50.

"World Was His Oyster," review of *The Founding Father: The Story of Joseph P. Kennedy* by Richard J. Whalen, *National*

Review, 1 December 1964, pp. 1064–1066.

"Questions About the New Fiction." *National Review*, 30 November 1965, pp. 1100–1102.

"Big Rock Candy Figgy Pudding Pitfall." *Saturday Evening Post*, 3 December 1966, p. 22.

"In Praise of Unhung Wreaths and Love." *Life*, 19 December 1969, p. 213.

"On the Last Frontier With VX and GB." *Life*, 13 March 1970, p. 20.

"Why I Write," *New York Times Book Review*, 5 December 1976, p. 2.

Review of *Falconer* by John Cheever. *New York Times Book Review*, 6 March 1977, p. 1.

"Letter from Manhattan," review of *Manhattan*, *Interiors*, and *Annie Hall*. *New York Review of Books*, 16 August 1979, pp. 18–19.

"I Want to go Ahead and Do It," review of *The Executioner's Song* by Norman Mailer. *New York Times Book Review*, 7 October 1979, p. 1.

"Without Regret or Hope," review of *The Return of Eva Peron With the Killings in Trinadad* by V. F. Maipaul. *New York Review of Books*, 12 June 1980, pp. 20–21.

WORKS ABOUT JOAN DIDION

Braudy, Susan. "A Day in the Life of Joan Didion." *Ms.*, February 1977, p. 65.

Clemons, Walter. "Didion Country." *Newsweek*, 25 June 1979, pp. 84–85.

Davenport, Guy. "Midas' Grandchildren." *National Review*, 7 May 1963, p. 371.

Davidson, Sara. "A Visit With Joan Didion." *The New York Times Book Review*, 3 April 1971, p. 1.

Dinnage, Rosemary. "A Taste for Devastation." *Times Literary Supplement*, 30 November 1979, p. 52.

Duffy, Martha. "Pictures from an Expedition." *New York Times Book Review*, 16 August 1979, pp. 43–44.

Harrison, Barbara Grizzeti. "Joan Didion: The Courage of Her Afflictions." *Nation*, 29 September 1979, pp. 277–286.

Hulbert, Ann. "The White Album." *New Republic*, 23 June 1979, pp. 35–36.

"Imagination of Disaster." *Time*, 28 March 1977, pp. 87-88.

"Joan Didion." *Current Biography*. New York: H. W. Wilson Company, 1978, pp. 108-111.

Kakutani, Michiko. "Joan Didion: Staking Out California." *New York Times Magazine*, 10 June 1979, pp. 44-50.

Kazin, Alfred. "Joan Didion: Portrait of a Professional." *Harpers*, December 1971, pp. 112-114.

Lardner, Susan. "Facing Facts." *New Yorker*, 20 June 1977, pp. 117-118.

Leonard, John. "The Cities of the Desert, the Desert of the Mind." *New York Times*, 21 July 1970, p. 33.

MIM. "Slouching Towards Bethlehem." *Commonweal*, 29 November 1968, p. 324.

Morrow, Lance. "American Death Traps." *Time*, 20 August 1979, p. 69.

Oates, Joyce Carol. "A Taut Novel of Disorder." *New York Times Book Review*, 3 April 1977, p. 1.

Prescott, Peter S. "Didion's Grace." *Newsweek*, 21 March 1977, p. 81.

Raphael, Frederic. "Grace Under Pressure." *Saturday Review*, 5 March 1977, p. 23.

Romano, John. "Joan Didion and Her Characters." *Commentary*, July 1977, pp. 61-63.

Segal, Lore. "Play It As It Lays." *New York Times Book Review*, 9 August 1970, p. 6.

Shaw, Elizabeth Woods. "A Book of Common Prayer." *America*, 10 September 1977, pp. 135-136.

Shorer, Mark. "Novels and Nothingness." *American Scholar*, 40 (Winter 1970-71), pp. 168-174.

Stevenson, Catherine Barnes. "Film as Metaphor in Didion's *Play It As It Lays*." (Paper delivered at the Annual Spring Convention of the Northeast Modern Language Association, North Dartmouth, Mass., 21 March 1980).

Stimpson, Catherine. "The Case of Miss Joan Didion." *Ms.*, January 1973, pp. 36-41.

Towers, Robert, "The Decline and Fall of the 60's." *New York Times Book Review*, 17 June 1971, p. 1.

Wakefield, Dan. "Slouching Towards Bethlehem." *New York Times Book Review*, 21 July 1968, p. 8.

Wilson, James Q. "In California." *Commentary*, September 1979, pp. 79-80.

"Writer's Roost." *Vogue*, 1 October 1972, pp. 146-149.

Index

MODERN LITERATURE SERIES

In the same series (continued from page ii)

DATE